Start Your Own
Mail Order Lingerie
Business

PRENTICE HALL PRESS

ISBN 0-7352-0082-3

ATTENTION: CORPORATIONS AND SCHOOLS
Prentice Hall books are available at quantity discounts with bulk purchase for educational, business, or sales promotional use. For information, please write to: Prentice Hall Special Sales, 240 Frisch Court, Paramus, New Jersey 07652. Please supply: title of book, ISBN, quantity, how the book will be used, date needed.

PRENTICE HALL PRESS
Paramus, NJ 07652

On the World Wide Web at http://www.phdirect.com

CONTENTS

Preface

Start Your Own Mail Order Lingerie Business is the result of many hours of in-depth research into one of the fastest growing opportunities in home-based business today. Our exclusive team of National Business Library's professional business writers has brought years of practical experience to this project, and we know that the information provided in this book will set you on the road to success.

Owning your own business can be the most exciting and rewarding venture you will ever experience. We talk of hundreds of small business owners who make comments like, "Doing something I really enjoy makes every day a pleasure," or "If I had known I would be realizing this kind of income, rather than making my former boss wealthy, I would have started my own business years ago."

It's true! You'll never get rich working for someone else. By capitalizing on your experience, investing time and energy, and studying the proven techniques and business methods provided in this book, you will be well on the way to realizing your goals for success in your own venture. It takes courage to begin. Without a doubt, the first step is the hardest–and you have already taken it.

INTRODUCTION:
THE LEATHER AND LACE REVOLUTION

Mail order is no longer a secondary trend; it's an established way of doing business. Big business. Statistics continue to show staggering revenues generated in this industry: 30 percent of all Americans purchased items through the mail and spent an unprecedented 70 billion dollars last year alone. Add another 55 billion for magazine subscriptions, record and book clubs, and home shopping networks and you can see just how profitable this business has become.

Why is mail order such a promising venture? This industry has been around for well over a hundred years (Montgomery Ward, the grand-daddy of mail order, was founded in 1872), but now thanks to changes in people's attitudes toward mail order, better service by mail order companies, and advances in technology, it has become a mainstay in how consumers purchase goods of all kinds—from appliances to eyeglasses and pianos to pencils.

But where can a new business operator stake his or her claim in the wide-ranging landscape of mail order? Our research has shown that one of the best places to start is in the lingerie field. It's a proven fact that lingerie has, and always will be, one of the top revenue producers in the mail order industry—outselling computers, appliances, toys or even books and compact disks.

Selling lingerie by itself is a prime start-up business because of its simplicity: minimal experience, if any, is necessary to begin, the initial start-up costs can be very low compared to other businesses, and the return on investment is usually very quick.

And since lingerie is a necessity for many consumers and is also a consumable good (i.e., constantly used and needing to be replaced—underwear, bras, panties, camisoles and hosiery) the demand for these products will never diminish. Lingerie isn't a fad or a trend; these are average everyday items that will always be around—and be sold.

Selling lingerie through the mail takes into account all of these aspects and provides solutions to some of the problems faced by retail operators and lingerie buyers alike.

Everyone is familiar with the "embarrassment factor" of walking into a retail lingerie shop or the lingerie section of a department store (this is especially true for men who might be gift shopping). Women don't enjoy trying on personal products in small, cramped changing stalls under the scrutiny of fluorescent lights, nagging salespeople or video cameras—along with the added uncertainty that some of these items might have been tried on by tens or hundreds of others. Mail order changes all of this.

By providing lingerie and other personal items directly to the consumer's home, the privacy and the anonymity aspects now make buying a pleasure. Women can see what they, and the garments, look like in the right conditions—

at home—and men will become more willing to buy not only special gifts for their spouses or girlfriends, but purchase some of the available men's underwear and lounge wear also.

Dealing with purchasing lingerie from home has become more convenient in recent years than even going to a neighborhood shop or nearby department store. This is true mainly because of the seemingly unlimited sizes and styles that mail order provides along with the speed of delivery. Most mail order lingerie sellers will use Federal Express, UPS or some other overnight service to guarantee prompt delivery. You should keep this in mind when you reach the point at which you're planning the fulfillment and shipping part of your business. People are now expecting promptness, and this will be an edge over your competition if you're willing and able to provide it.

As far as running the business goes, one of the major pluses is the autonomy you'll have. Mail order lingerie really lends itself well to entrepreneurs who like to work at their own speed—not just in day-to-day operation, but in the planning of capital expenses, increasing of inventory, hiring, and personal involvement. You may want to do it all and work 16 hours a day or just oversee a few employees and work part of the day. And as we stated earlier, you can easily work from a small area: your home, a small office or even just a desk!

As you've proven by buying this business guide, you're serious about your future. And by the content of this book, you see yourself pursuing a career in mail order lingerie—following in the footsteps of multi-million dollar companies like Frederick's of Hollywood and Victoria's Secret.

Mail order lingerie is a very specialized and glamorous business. The profit margins are high, providing excellent income potential and business longevity—yet for all the enticing and complex features it has to offer, it's rooted in simplicity. It is a constantly growing industry that can offer exciting new arenas for expanding the market and increasing your product lines and revenue.

After studying this business guide you will know the innermost secrets and intricacies of this highly successful business and be well on your way to an exciting and new opportunity—being your own boss in the cash rich industry of mail order lingerie!

1

THE GROWTH OF
SMALL BUSINESS

The 1980s were referred to as America's "entrepreneurial era." In 1986, more than 750,000 new businesses were created in the United States. In 1989, more than a million new ventures were started nationwide - almost half of them by women. In 1991, there were 20.5 million small businesses in the United States - and the entrepreneurial era is continuing through the 1990s. The recession of the early 1990s compelled suddenly unemployed people to start their own businesses in order to survive. An upsurge in part-time businesses has also fueled an entrepreneurial trend, with people in search of extra income working on profitable ventures during their off hours.

More and more people are opting to leave their 9-to-5 jobs and stop "making someone else" rich to focus their energies on building a successful business of their own. The combined circumstances of fewer advancement opportunities, lack of job security, and the possibility of retiring without a pension are also driving the trend toward self-employment.

Today, the number of individuals who are self-employed is at its highest level ever, and based on your interest in this book, it's quite possible that you'll be joining the ranks of small business owners in the near future. It may be simply a dream right now, but that's how these businesses start.

Starting and operating your own small business is one of the most exciting and satisfying challenges you can undertake. There are no limitations on income potential when you're investing time and energy in your own enterprise. With the practical information provided in this book and dedication to your business goals, your chances for success are excellent.

What Is a Small Business?

The majority of businesses in the United States today are classified as small business. The definitions of what constitutes a small business run the gamut from the size of the overall staff (typically under 100) to the amount of assets or sales volume. However, in this book, small business is defined as one that is independently owned and operated.

The major benefit of this type of business is that you have the ability to make decisions quickly and act on them immediately. What typically bogs down big business is the number of people involved in the decision-making process.

Other advantages include the fact that small businesses can provide personalized service to the community or the market they're serving and the owner has the freedom, independence, and control to operate exactly as he or she chooses.

It's important to remember, however, that most major

corporations, from Ford Motor Company and McDonald's to Mary Kay Cosmetics, started out as small businesses - as dreams.

It was because of basic business sense and a willingness to learn and adapt as their companies grew that Henry Ford, Ray Kroc, and Mary Kay, and thousands like them, steered their dreams into monumental financial successes.

Whether your goal is to supplement an existing income and to operate a solely owned home-based business from your garage, kitchen table, or spare bedroom, or to start a business that involves raising substantial capital, finding and setting up a commercial location, and hiring employees, you have the potential to enjoy an independent lifestyle that carries with it a number of rewards. And the rewards are as varied as the people who pursue them.

Accepting the Challenge

Remember, these rewards do not come without hard work and the willingness to research and understand all facets of running your business. Many new businesses fail within the first few years.

Reasons given for the early demise of a small business range from lack of organization or management experience to undercapitalization, misunderstanding of the importance of advertising, inexperience in pricing products and services, lack of an overall business plan, improper hiring practices, and failure to accurately assess the competition.

It isn't that someone purposely starts a business without having explored these areas. However, many times a person feels that his or her demonstrated expertise while in the employ of another can easily be transferred into a personal business. This is only partially true.

While it is imperative that you have particular skills or talents - because selling them is what your ultimate success will be based on - it's equally important to understand how to sell them, to know exactly what your profit margin is, and what steps you need to take to ensure the continued growth of your business.

Sounds easy, right? It really can be. But like anything else worth doing, starting your own business means careful planning. For example, you wouldn't consider taking a month-long vacation without doing some serious planning to ensure that the house was taken care of while your were gone, that you had made reservations for lodging, tours,and flights, and that you had converted your cash into traveler's checks.

There are so many aspects involved in running a business, it is vital to be prepared for any eventuality. Being prepared means being informed, so that when situations do arise you know how to deal with them.

Is "Failure" Really Failure?

We have all heard stories about people who started their businesses on a shoestring and who became successful because of their sheer determination to make it work. It does happen, but these people are the exception rather than the rule, and in most cases have had experts standing behind them to give them guidance when problems came up. Others fail and, unfortunately, this often holds potential new business owners back. We hear and read about amazingly high figures related to so-called business failures.

According to a research project conducted by Albert Shapero, professor of the American Free Enterprise System at Ohio State University for many years, no one really knows the true failure rate of new businesses. The main reason for this is because there is not really a standard definition of "failure" in this case. He points out that a number of businesses close for a variety of reasons, many of which are not documented.

For example, in some cases the owners reach retirement age and have no one to pass the business along to; others shut down because the owners simply get bored; while still other entrepreneurs file a Chapter 11 bankruptcy, which basically gives them the opportunity to stay in business and continue operating under a court-approved plan, even though they become a statistic on the "failure" list.

The other extremely important aspect to consider when thinking about the benefits and risks of starting your own business is that having a business fail has never been a deterrent for true entrepreneurs. Many well-known business moguls failed at least once, and often more than once, before striking it rich.

Learning from Experience

In fact, almost anyone who has had a business fail will tell you that the experience was more valuable than anything they could have been taught in a business school, and that it provided them with the knowledge they needed to start another venture successfully. This kind of determination is a valid qualification for self-employment and will pay off handsomely.

When you own your own business, you are responsible for everything. There will be times, such as when your accounts receivable are running sixty days late or the phone company puts the wrong number in your Yellow Pages listing, when returning to the 9-to-5 world will seem like a tempting option.

This is where self-discipline, an unwavering belief in your product or service, and the determination to be your own boss will pull you through.

But, again, we can't stress enough the importance of planning, understanding basic business practices, being aware of consumer trends, and taking the time to develop, implement, and update goals to ensure success for your efforts.

What This Book Offers

This book is designed to provide you with the information you will need to start your Mail Order Lingerie business, to offer techniques to help you with day-to-day operations, and to provide anecdotes about people just like you who had a dream and, through planning and determination, were able to turn that dream into a successful reality.

In addition to focusing on aspects of the Mail Order Lingerie business, we cover such important business matters as:

- Recognizing the entrepreneurial profile
- Taking our exclusive Entrepreneurial Quiz
- Finding the right audience for your business through easy marketing techniques
- Organizing for efficiency
- Recognizing legalities
- Addressing financial concerns
- Getting your home office up and running
- Charting your enterprise's growth

You will find specific how-to information on:

- Advertising and promoting your business
- Finding capital
- Saving money on operating expenses
- Developing a simple bookkeeping system that will show you whether you're facing a financial crisis or realizing a profit

You're never too young, too old, too busy, or too poor to start a business. Owning your own business means taking advantage of our marvelous system of free enterprise. Earning a substantial living and, even better, realizing a profit for doing something that you enjoy is the American dream come true.

The opportunities for entrepreneurs have never been better. Armed with a solid product or service to sell, the determination to succeed and, most important, business know-how, there is nothing that can stand in your way.

Notes

Key Points:

_____

_____

_____

_____

Personal Thoughts:

_____

_____

_____

_____

_____

_____

_____

_____

Additional Research:

_____

_____

_____

_____

2

THE RIGHT STUFF: THE ENTREPRENEURIAL PROFILE

Starting a business is one thing: making it work is another. We know that success in self-employment is largely the result of careful planning and understanding basic business techniques and formulas.

It is equally important that you start a business based on your expertise in a specific field and focused on your involvement in an area that you thoroughly enjoy. As many successful entrepreneurs claim, making money doing something you love is the best way to ensure a profitable future. It is always easier to address the inevitable business challenges that crop up when you are, at bottom line, creating a product or providing a service that gives you a sense of pleasure and personal satisfaction.

Personality is also a factor in determining what kind of business to get involved in, the way you will eventually set up the legal structure (sole proprietorship, partnership, etc.) and how you will run the business on a day-to-day basis. For example, if you are planning to start a business that is based on your artistic or creative abilities, it is possible that your personality is not suited to the very important aspect of sales. But without strong selling abilities there is a likelihood that your goal of distributing, for example, your hand-carved wooden boxes nationally will not come to fruition.

This isn't to say that you should decide against going into business for yourself. It simply indicates it would be in your best interest to join forces with someone who does have strong selling skills, who believes in the product as much as you do and will work toward a common goal.

On the other hand, if your personality is geared to working with people, it is a good idea to consider a business that will emphasize this ability, such as developing seminars or workshops based on your area of expertise, providing independent counseling or tutoring, or a service such as gift basket designing, which depends on your interaction with people on a one-to-one or on a group basis for success.

Self-motivation, otherwise known as drive, is one of the most important personality traits of successful entrepreneurs. This is the characteristic that gets you going and keeps you moving when you are in business for yourself. It's what helps you to keep turning out those craft items, upgrading your technical skills or developing new and improved promotional techniques when business is slow. It's what gives you the tenacity and confidence to call on a potential client even though they have told you "No" three times.

Self-motivation is also what helps you overcome the fears and concerns that inevitably arise when you own your own business. It is the main ingredient that has spurred on those people we hear about who have achieved success despite drawbacks, such as minimal capital, lack of education or limited experience.

People with a high degree of self-motivation see the greatest obstacles, such as learning a new aspect of business management, as a new and exciting challenge to overcome. If you've ever undertaken a project without fully understanding the mechanics involved in performing the task or knowing what the outcome would be, you were operating on self-motivation—the conviction that you would be able to learn whatever needed to be done to accomplish your goal.

And regardless of the outcome of the project, you undoubtedly gained more experience and knowledge than you had before, which only works to increase your sense of motivation to handle new challenges.

Research shows that the true entrepreneur should possess the following kinds of personality traits in order to be able to address the many and varied situations that arise in business ownership:

Ten Traits of Successful Entrepreneurs

1. Motivation
(Self-driven, goal-oriented)

2. Confidence
(Belief in oneself & one's goals)

3. Self-Awareness
(Cognizance of one's positives & negatives)

4. Courage
(Separates the entrepreneur from the dreamer)

5. Curiosity
(The constant need to increase awareness)

6. Optimism
(Expectant, forward-looking)

7. Flexibility
(Adaptable to changing needs)

8. Decisiveness
(Able to make quick, wise decisions)

9. Patience
(With people as well as circumstances)

10. Drive
(The unquenchable desire to succeed)

The willingness to take risks. Courage is a valuable trait when striving for success. We have heard successful people say something similar to this: "I don't know how I did it; I just made a phone call and asked for the money I needed." It was more than luck that made it possible for this person to raise the capital they needed to get their business off the ground; it was the willingness to take a chance—in this case, the risk that they would receive a positive response to the request.

The owner of a small cabinet-refinishing business said, "I always figure that the worst thing that can happen is someone will say no, so it never hurts to try." In the game of business, you must be willing to take chances. Even if you don't get exactly what you want every time, the odds are good that if you feel strongly about what you need, you will get it. But you have to ask!

Confidence. The age-old philosophy of positive thinking is a step in the direction of success. By behaving as if you already are a success at what you do, it follows that you will be, and your customers will believe it too. A confident attitude is one of the most appealing traits you can exhibit to a prospective client, for it lets them know that they will be getting the best their money can buy.

Patience. When you own your own business, there will be moments when you feel as if the roof is caving in, especially when your suppliers seem to be taking their own sweet time in fulfilling an important order or when a customer's demands seem to be unrealistic. Although you may be able to hurry the supplier along, you must remember that your customers are always right, since they are the ones who can financially make or break your business.

If you are aware that patience is not a strong suit, develop a stop-gap exercise for yourself to use at times when coping is a definite necessity. Whether its the time-honored "count to ten before saying a word" theory, visualizing a pleasant scene or repeating a secret phrase to yourself when tension is running high, it will be to your advantage.

Decision-making. Business has been described as a process of making one fast decision after another. Often, a decision has to be made immediately, on the spur of the moment. In those instances, you should go with your intuition and trust that you are doing the right thing.

However, if you are the type of person who prefers to analyze your options, weigh all the factors and make decisions slowly, then that is what you must do. It will not only keep your confidence intact, but will ensure that you're taking the right action. Again, careful planning will help you predict many of the decision-making situations arising in business. As time goes by and you grow more comfortable in your role as business owner, you'll find yourself making faster decisions.

> *You have to accept whatever comes, and the important thing is that you meet it with courage and with the best you have to give.*
>
> *Eleanor Roosevelt*

Experience. The results of a Dun & Bradstreet survey conducted a few years back indicated that a primary reason some businesses fail within a few years of start-up is "incompetence in the area of business experience." Whether or not your experience is directly related to the business you're planning to start, it's a key component for growth.

If you feel you don't have enough business experience, there are several avenues you can take before starting your own enterprise. Returning to school for specialized courses is one answer. Most community colleges and adult education facilities offer classes and seminars in business start-up and maintenance these days. There are also hundreds of courses available to you by mail—over 1,200 schools and universities now offer home study or correspondence courses that will, in many cases, give you official certification in your field.

However, your best solution is to take a job in the field

you're interested in. By asking questions about all aspects of the business, you will gain experience, get paid for learning and find out whether this is really what you want to do—before sinking money, time and energy into the enterprise.

Perseverance. One of the adages you will hear time and time again when talking to entrepreneurs is that perseverance is 90 percent of the battle to succeed. If you are like the majority of new small business owners, the entire staff and support system for your venture is probably you. Making a dream come true can be a lonely task, especially when you are just getting started, and ensuring that it works often means little rest or relaxation. You must be willing to persevere during the rough times, to hang in there during the slow periods and to maintain your belief in your product and service even when it seems like no one else in the world knows you exist. It has been written that through perseverance the snail reached the ark. So it is with success!

The Entrepreneurial A to Z Appraisal

Owning a business calls for the ability to handle different situations with confidence. The following self-appraisal quiz has no right or wrong answers. It is designed to help you in determining personality traits, attitudes and qualifications that will benefit you in your venture.

The Entrepreneurial Quiz

Use the letter *S* for strong or *N* for needs improvement beside the characteristics listed below. Give yourself sufficient time to analyze each trait. Upon completion, use the appraisal as a starting point for discussions with friends and family members about your business profile. Acknowledging the strong and weak points will help you prepare for your role as an entrepreneur.

Achievement: I have a strong desire to be successful in my chosen business venture.   _____

Belief: I have a faith in myself and the service or product I am specializing in to build my business.   _____

Creativity: I am able to address situations in imaginative and innovative ways to reach my goals.   _____

Discipline: I am self-motivated and able to handle necessary tasks, whether or not I enjoy them.   _____

Efficient: I am organized and able to arrange my priorities or change my work methods as needed for maximum production.   _____

Friendly: I am genuinely interested in people and enjoy my interactions with them on a day-to-day basis.   _____

Goal-Oriented: I have a tendency to set my sights on preset goals and to work hard toward them.   _____

Health-Conscious: I am aware of my physical abilities and have the insight to work smart in order to preserve my health.   _____

Independent: I am able to work alone, if necessary, and prefer to be responsible for my own actions. ____

Judgment: My conclusions about people or situations are generally accurate. ____

Knowledge: I have solid experience in my field and have spent enough time in a professional business setting to learn the ropes. ____

Leadership: I am able to direct people effectively while instilling confidence and loyalty. ____

Maturity: I am willing to work toward long-term goals and do not get upset by the inevitable minor setbacks. ____

Networking: I am willing to develop associations with other entrepreneurs for bilateral support in my venture. ____

Optimism: I am able to see what is right about a situation and to explore its potential to the fullest. ____

Positive Attitude: I am convinced that I can accomplish anything I decide to do and rarely entertain negative thoughts. ____

Questioning: I am not afraid to ask questions to get the information I need to expand my knowledge. ____

Resourceful: I am able to find ways to accomplish just about any task I must do. ____

Sales Ability: I can present information about myself and/or my business in a convincing yet honest manner. ____

Tolerance: I am able to handle stressful situations with a positive and realistic attitude. ____

Undaunted Spirit: I am unafraid of the unknown. In fact, I enjoy a challenge and accept the consequences of my actions. ____

Venturesome: I am not afraid of hard work to reach my goals and enjoy finding new, positive ways to handle troublesome situations. ____

Well-balanced: I generally maintain a sense of humor when things don't work out as expected. ____

Expressive: I am able to express ideas and feelings, both orally and in written form, with clarity and logic. ____

Youthful Nature: I am capable of tackling work with enthusiasm and a high level of energy. ____

Zest: I look forward to enjoying my business, the people I will be dealing with and the resulting fruits of my labor. ____

Scoring

Although this is not a test, merely a tool to provide you with information about your entrepreneurial profile, there are immediate clues to your future as a business owner in the responses you have given.

If you have indicated 15 or more S codes, there is a good possibility that you have been involved in your own business in the past or, at least, have worked in a managerial capacity for someone else. You have the positive personality traits required to be a successful business owner. If you have between 8 and 15 S responses, you are basically a positive and directed person and should not have any problem with improving certain areas to increase your personal business success potential.

If you have fewer than 8 S responses, this is an indication that finding a complimentary business partner who can support your goals may be an option worth considering.

3

MAIL ORDER LINGERIE: FROM HOMESTEADING TO HOME PROFIT

Glamorous, sexy, seductive and sensible. All of these words describe the world of lingerie. And better yet, they describe the business side of mail order also. This booming industry is still growing and there is plenty of room on the "ground floor" for many entrepreneurs ready to start. It's an exciting time and being able to sell exciting products only enhances your ability to cash in on some big profit potential. It is important, however, to understand where mail order lingerie began in order to gain some insight as to where it's going.

Way Back When

When mail order pioneers first set out to supply people with a way to purchase items through the mail (many homesteaders, farmers and small town residents had no way of shopping for basic consumer goods during the

1800s and 1900s without traveling an average of 90 miles to the nearest "department" store), they knew that basic necessities would surely be the most in demand. What they didn't realize was how large the demand of women who wanted their own necessities—lingerie—would be.

Next to household wares, tools and farm equipment, lingerie and women's items were right at the top of the list. Everything from plain cotton nightgowns to fancy French lace underwear was now made available direct to the home, and the demand was overwhelming. And why not? Women were primarily relegated to the household duties such as washing, cooking and cleaning, yet on average were better educated than their male counterparts. They were first to see the catalogs and understand the importance of not having to travel great distances for basic necessities—usually in limited supply. They generally ran the household and understood the savings of time and energy—not to mention the bargains to be had in buying supplies through mail order.

Familiar companies like Sears & Roebuck and Montgomery Ward started out as small general stores, no different from hundreds like them across the country, but they found an important niche in the market—supplying everyone everywhere with what they needed using the help of the U.S. Post Office and other carriers. And what started as a simple idea soon built these local merchants into the giants of mail order. But let's not forget that a lot of this growth had to do with the demand by women for women's products—especially lingerie.

As it was then and is now, lingerie mail order has been a major portion of the entire mail order arena and has grown substantially in the last few years. Take any clothing or department store catalog you've received in the mail recently and look at how lingerie and undergarment pages are positioned (usually in the front section and covering quite a few pages).

A recent 600-page Speigel® catalog (which sells just about everything from tennis shoes to teapots) devoted 42% of its catalog to women's clothing and more than 11% of that was all lingerie and related items. You can see how big the presence of lingerie is when you compare that to the 2.3% of space used for all of the men's fashions and accessories. And it doesn't stop there—Sears, J.C. Penney, Chadwick's, J. Crew, Ann Taylor, even Eddie Bauer and L.L. Bean are following suit. Most full-service mail order clothing companies know the benefit of providing lingerie—and so will you.

Your Interests

You obviously chose this book because you were interested in starting your own lingerie mail order business. You have an attraction to, and probably a good knowledge of, lingerie and its profit potential, but haven't had the precise resources to do anything about it. You've seen the catalogs show up at your house—glamorous models in sultry poses lounging around wearing chic, seductive, or just plain, functional undergarments. There's a universal allure and mystique that accompanies this industry, along with an air of sophistication and "big" money. You've seen it all from the outside; now you'll learn the secrets and soon become one of the "insiders."

This guide will introduce you to the many aspects involved in starting and running your mail order lingerie business: finding suppliers, allocating inventory space, setting up your office, keeping an eye out for "what's hot" and preparing for quick expansion. The lingerie business isn't for everyone. You need to have a true desire for, and interest in, the inner-workings of lingerie mail order and the willingness to be successful—and so far, it looks like you're on the right path!

Good Growth

Mail order lingerie is enjoying a continued growth rate averaging 5 to 15% yearly and is proving that there is plenty of room for new companies to stake their claim. One trend that has become apparent is that many lingerie companies are expanding and including a lot of non-lingerie items. This is good for them but better for you.

By limiting the exposure of lingerie in marketing pieces such as catalogs, the demand for "strictly lingerie" catalogs is increasing. This is where the best chance for success exists right now. For example, the latest Victoria's Secret catalog used less than 40% of its pages to promote lingerie. Sounds surprising, but it's true. Now that they're

Overview of Mail Order Lingerie

This is a labor-intensive business with strong income potential and steady growth. It does not lend itself to absentee ownership and can be started from home with the owner as sole employee.

Minimum Start-up Investment:	$3,500
Average Start-up Investment:	$7,500
High Start-up Investment:	$15,000-$50,000
Breakeven Point:	Three months to one year
Average Annual Gross Revenues:	$60,000-$150,000
Potential Annual Gross Revenues:	$250,000+

expanding into the clothing and accessories market, they're leaving behind a gap that initially made them famous. Who will fill this niche in the market and become the next big lingerie success? You will!

Don't forget—even though lingerie is considered glamorous, sexy or exotic, it is still very much a necessity for most consumers and will always have a captive audience waiting for newer, more comfortable, more chic, more erotic and more unique items to add to their wardrobes.

Seductive Simplicity

What makes mail order lingerie an enticing business can be summed up in one word: simplicity. Lingerie demand, lingerie supply and the running of a lingerie business are based almost entirely on the concept of simplicity.

It's important to have a good conceptual idea of what it is you'll be doing as far as owning and operating a mail order lingerie business. First and foremost, we'll expand on the "simplicity" aspects of how the business flows in terms of demand, supply and the daily running of operations.

Simplicity in Captivity

Knowing right off that you have a large, eager and captive audience of consumers waiting to purchase your lingerie products overcomes a major hurdle. Many businesses, both established and entrepreneurial, risk a lot of money, time and energy trying to sell products that the general public either isn't familiar with or just doesn't want. By dealing with a product or service that isn't deemed a necessity to cost-conscious buyers, the odds of being successful can weigh heavily against you. Thankfully, this won't be a problem for you.

As far as the lingerie market is concerned, there are three basic types of lingerie consumers: those that primarily want functionality (basic, plain, comfortable underwear); those that want exotic and erotic accessory types of lingerie (open-bust teddies, leather and lace merry-widows, sheer sequined body-suits) and the large audience whose tastes fall in between (charmeuse camisoles, silk boxers, lace panties, etc).

You can see how different catalogs market each one of these segments: Hanes/Legg's puts out a catalog that reaches the first market (good brand name functional bras, panties, hosiery and slips); Frederick's of Hollywood focuses on the more exotic and seductive (leather g-strings, feather boas, peek-a-boo baby-dolls); while Victoria's Secret aims for those in the middle (lace gowns, silk kimonos, designer bras and panties).

Know Your Functional Buyers

No one can argue the necessity of good quality underwear—comfortable and durable for both men and women. On the broad side of lingerie/undergarment demand are the basics: cotton briefs, panties, bras, slips and hosiery. To many, these items are merely afterthoughts; not much time is generally spent on shopping for and choosing the best quality and comfort, let alone searching for the best values. By providing a way for consumers to actually see, shop and compare many articles of undergarments in one place (with a catalog, flyer or booklet) more emphasis can be placed on the informed buying of these items. What was once secondary will now be a more qualified consideration.

Supplying the basics will be your "bread and butter." This segment of consumers will be the most steady and predictable. You'll be able to count on the demand from this group—making profit forecasts, inventory allotment and seasonal changes all that much easier to count on.

Stepping Them Up

You might consider the functional buyer segment enough to concentrate on, but you shouldn't stop there. By giving buyers the opportunity to move from the basic needs of underwear to the desire for more stylish and accented versions of lingerie, you'll be increasing awareness and capitalize from it. Cotton is comfortable, but for a little more money who wouldn't want silk or charmeuse? By covering the entire gamut of lingerie, your catalog or brochures will upsell on their own. This encompasses the next group of undergarment buyers—those who want the necessities, but with a little more flair or comfort.

As you negotiate with your manufacturers and wholesalers, you'll see the marginal cost differences between the basics and the "premier" items offered. It will be your job to price products accordingly—any "premium" or "deluxe" item should carry a "premium" or "deluxe" price. You're offering better quality and value, so make the profit margins count.

Something Wild

Ask anyone what they think of when they hear the word lingerie. The responses will be as varied as the actual products, but one thing will remain—the sex factor. For most, there is that underlying mystique and sensuality that will always be tied to lingerie, which is exactly why you should be in this business—sex sells. And sexy lingerie sells a lot.

With psychologists and psychiatrists prescribing numerous "treatments" for relationship and self-esteem problems, one item in particular seems to constantly be in vogue: lingerie. It's becoming more and more popular for men and women of all ages, persuasions and body types to indulge in using glamorous and sensual lingerie to enhance attractiveness and interest in modern day relationships.

This segment of the market routinely demands the more detailed, intricate and luxurious types of lingerie to fulfill any sort of want for fantasy, attraction and mystique. Because of this demand, the pricing of these items are generally higher, building in a sure-fire profit margin for you. As you'll see from some of the catalogs you'll order (see Resources section at the end of this book) the range of materials, configurations and looks is staggering. Leather, lace, fishnet, chain and even rubber may not be your cup of tea, but from the sales standpoint, these items generate a lot of money.

Simple Supply

On the supply side, there are a number of lingerie manu-facturers and wholesalers willing and able to supply you with top quality lingerie. Some are more specialized than others. You will need to decide your market mix (which of the three consumer types you want to primarily focus on), then shop around for the best value and service. Again, simplicity: find the right suppliers for what you need. (We've already done most of that research for you in our Resources section! We want to start you off right and help you be successful).

When initially talking to suppliers, have a list of ques-tions ready and get as much information as possible. You're going to want to compare prices, selection and availability among all of your potential suppliers to find out who has the best quality and service at the lowest price. Don't be afraid to negotiate. Most wholesalers and manufacturers offer quantity discounts or a percentage off the price if you pay up front. These savings will add up to give you an edge over your competition.

You'll also want to find out about shipping charges, drop-shipping, credit accounts, location and related lingerie products. By having a separate script of all these questions for each supplier you talk to, and filling in the answers, you will more easily be able to compare the pluses and minuses and decide on the best wholesalers and manufacturers to use. These questionnaires will also act as backup should you need to change to a different supplier for any reason. (A more complete look at the supply line and specific questions can be found in the Operations section of this book).

The Business Routine

As far as running the business is concerned, your main objective is to supply the demand. You notify your customers that you're selling lingerie; they respond by placing orders; you send them the merchandise. There are specifics to each step, but this is basically all there is to running a mail order lingerie, or any other mail order business, for that matter.

Notifying customers that you're selling lingerie is another way of describing marketing. It includes producing your product materials (catalogs, brochures, flyers, sales letters) and the promotion of the business (direct mailing, advertising, press releases, etc.). Marketing will be the way you get the word out that you have a wide selection of top quality lingerie at great prices. You'll be sending catalogs directly to customers from lingerie mailing lists that you get from list brokers and running ads for people to send for a catalog. You'll produce a press release to send to local and regional TV and radio stations for publicity and mail out an introduction letter to various clubs and organizations. Now that you're in business, you have to set the marketing wheels in motion. Let the public know what you have, where you are, and the best way to reach you.

Once the buying community knows what you have to offer, you will receive orders. How are you going to handle the processing of these orders? Don't panic. There are many ways to process your orders. You might have customers send them directly to you by mail or phone, depending on the quantity you're able to handle. A manual system of recording orders will work fine in the beginning, but won't be that practical as the business expands. An inexpensive computer and invoicing software can take you to the next level just fine. Your highest option would be to use a professional answering service that can operate 24 hours a day using an 800 number and supply you with a complete list of orders daily. (When you start calculating the time it takes for you to do these functions, you might find that this option is the least expensive.)

Panties, bras, baby dolls, teddiettes, garters, chemises— no matter what the focus of your business, when the orders come in, you'd better have inventory or know where to get it.

By planning your business focus, calculating your start-up costs, figuring the capital that you have to work with, and talking to suppliers, you'll have a good idea as to what you'll need as far as inventory is concerned. You'll know from your suppliers whether they can get you products quickly, should you decide to rely on a just-in-time strategy (ordering the products as you receive the orders from customers), or give you the option of drop-shipping (you give your supplier the order and they ship directly to the customer). These are two ways to supply customers with the products they've ordered while keeping your inventory costs down.

More to Come

These three functions have been simplified to provide you with some basic overview and to start you thinking critically about how your mail order lingerie business will operate. The Operations section of this book will go into greater detail about these areas and provide you with the best possible ideas and plans of attack to ensure your success!

Lingerie Profit Potential: Your "Bottom" Line

As we've shown, the mail order lingerie industry has exploded into a 50+ billion dollar a year concern, but what does that mean to you? What can you expect in terms of profit potential?

Because half of the lingerie industry is based on necessities for the consumer—bras, panties, hosiery, slips, etc.—and because most people would rather buy these personal undergarments in the privacy of their own home there will always be a continuous demand for mail order lingerie.

Lingerie is a basic necessity of dress for people of all personalities and walks of life—men (briefs, boxers, pouches, thongs) and women (teddies, baby dolls, garter belts, chemises), young, old and of all sizes. The spectrum is broad and lends itself well to expansion, but we suggest starting with a specialized or more narrow range of products to begin with—limiting the start-up investment you'll need and maximizing your profit.

You aren't the first mail order lingerie business and you won't be the last. The idea is to be the best. Always look for better ways to market and supply your products. Concentrate on being able to provide higher quality, faster delivery and lower prices. Even though you might be specializing in the beginning (selling "chemises only" or "silk lingerie only") it doesn't mean you shouldn't have the best selection of these items available to your buyers. Honestly providing value is the best way ensure your business longevity and to capitalize in this industry.

On the next page is a breakdown of average costs and sales information showing you where profit is made in the sale of specific lingerie items. (These figures are based on a conservative national average and can vary depending on region—your actual costs could be substantially lower due to location, availability and quantity discounts.)

Average Lingerie Cost/Sales/Profit Comparison for Selected Items

	Wholesale	Retail	Mail Order	Customer Saves	You Profit
Bras					
Cotton	2.25	9.95	4.95	5.00	2.70
Designer/Lace Padded	7.50	19.95	14.95	5.00	7.45
Lace Padded Strapless	8.50	21.95	15.95	6.00	7.45
Panties					
Cotton	1.95	4.95	3.95	1.00	2.00
Designer/Lace Accented	3.95	9.95	7.95	2.00	4.00
Silk Thong	5.95	12.95	9.95	3.00	4.00
Garter Belts					
Silk and Lace	6.95	14.95	10.95	4.00	4.00
Faux Leather w/studs	11.50	24.95	18.95	3.00	7.45
Chemises					
Satin Chemise	17.75	49.95	34.95	15.00	17.20
Silk Charmeuse Chemise	16.00	34.95	24.95	10.00	8.95
Miscellaneous Items					
Chiffon Robe	19.75	49.95	36.95	13.00	15.20
Charmeuse Sleepshirt	17.50	44.95	34.95	10.00	17.45
Satin Gloves	8.95	19.95	14.95	5.00	6.00
Silk "Peek-a-boo" bikini	6.25	12.95	9.95	3.00	3.70

Learning the Lingo

As with any business, there are terms that are specific to the mail order industry. Knowing these basics will greatly enhance your ability to communicate with others in the industry—suppliers, printers, manufacturers, shippers, etc.

ARO - After Receipt of Order. Used to indicate specific time after an order is received when it will be delivered.

Bulk Mail - A category of third class mail for advertising/circular material. Use requires minimum quantities of 200 pieces, or by the pound, as a permit.

Business Reply Mail - Where the addressee (you) guarantees postage costs. Requires a permit. Using this makes customer replies easy and will usually guarantee high response rates.

Bustier - A one-piece strapless bra covering the chest down through the midriff.

Charmeuse - A soft, lightweight, satin-like cloth.

Chemise - An undergarment, somewhat like a loose, short slip or long undershirt, worn by women.

Chiffon - A sheer, silk material used primarily for women's apparel.

Cleaning - Where a mailing list is tested to eliminate unusable names.

COD - Cash On Delivery. A method of shipping products in which the carrier collects payment for the item at the point of delivery.

Column Inch - Refers to ad space one inch high by one column width. Space ad rates are computed by this unit of measurement.

Copy - Any advertising text, photos or line art.

Copyright - Status granted by law that establishes ownership and certain rights relating to published work.

Cover wrap - In printing, using a full color (4 color) printed piece as a cover that is bound to usually single or two color body pages. The cover wrap is primarily printed separately and on a different type of paper than the inside pages.

Dead Names - Names invalidated because person no longer lives at the address on the mailing list.

Direct Mail - Where advertising is sent directly to prospective buyers, either requested or from a list.

Display Ad - An ad bound with a border placed in print media (newspapers, magazines) usually with photos and sell-copy.

Drop Ship - Where you give a manufacturer names and payment, and he ships his products to customers under your name; or when you have an arrangement with a mail order house that includes your product in their catalog and mails orders to you to be filled.

4 Color - A printing term used to identify the four-ink process of printing that makes up almost all color print. Cyan, magenta, yellow and black inks are printed over, giving the illusion of continuous color.

In-House - Describes the performance of a specific task (usually farmed out or performed by an outside business or agency) done entirely within the company. One example would be that up until recently, many companies used advertising agencies to produce print ads. Now thanks to technology, companies are able to produce their own advertising "in-house" at a greatly reduced cost.

Insertion - When your ad appears in a publication (results from an insertion order).

JIT - Just In Time. An inventory control and supply method popularized by the Japanese. The idea is to be linked well enough with a supplier and have shipping time calculated so that when you receive an order for any given product, it is quickly passed to the supplier who in turn immediately ships it to you—reducing the need for inventory space and costs.

Key or Key Code - A code number put on any advertising material used to track where responses come from and when.

Line Art - Single color composition of lines, dots or shapes used in printed material, mainly advertising and editorial.

List Broker - Someone in the business of procuring and making available mailing lists comprised of names specific to a region, type or history.

Mailing List - A list from which you draw names and addresses of prospective customers, used for direct mail efforts.

Market Research - A formal or informal study of how well the public will receive a product or service.

Media - All the sources that you can utilize for advertising: magazines, newspapers, radio, television, posters, packaging, etc.

Merry Widow - A woman's undergarment combining a strapless bra and a boned corsette panty.

Optimum Price - Selling price that produces the highest net profit for any particular item in a market.

Overhead - All of your business expenses beyond the costs of production or supplies for the products or services you offer.

"Peek-a-boo" - A term used to describe lingerie that doesn't cover either the chest or crotch or both, or can be easily converted to do so.

Point of Diminishing Returns - As advertising space increases (as for a product in a catalog), so do overall revenues for that product. The point of diminishing returns is the point at which profit, based on space size, is maximized and starts to fall.

ROI - Return On Investment. Term used to identify time or cost involved to break even.

Self-Mailer - A mailed advertising piece that can be sent without an envelope; generally a catalog or folded brochure.

Sell-copy - Advertising text emphasizing the need to purchase an item, usually in an overly excited way. (Save Now! Huge Inventory At Drastically Reduced Prices! This Is Your Last Chance! are some examples).

Teddy - A woman's one-piece undergarment consisting of a top combined with loose-fitting drawers (bottoms).

Teddiette - A woman's one-piece undergarment consisting of a top combined with tight-fitting drawers (bottoms) usually small and bikini-like.

Testimonial - Words of praise from a satisfied customer, used in advertising.

Testing - The process of measuring responses for any change in marketing or production for a particular product.

2 Color - A printing term used to identify a printing process limited to two ink colors—usually black plus another color. This is most common in newspaper or phone book advertising.

4

MARKETING YOUR MAIL ORDER LINGERIE BUSINESS

How will you present your business to customers? Who will be the best audience to purchase your products? How will you know if you're succeeding? Beyond the scope of general marketing principles, mail order lingerie is truly based in research, testing, measuring and retesting.

Who's Doing What and Why?

Starting fresh in any business requires you to find your niche, or place in the market, on the best assumptions possible. By just deciding "I'm going to sell teddies and fishnet stockings only" can be setting yourself up for disaster.

The first task is to analyze the market. Find out what all, or as much of, the competition is doing and for how long. Using the resources available, gather all of the catalogs, brochures, mailers and other promotional material that the competition provides. Subscribe to catalogs and mailing lists that will send you lingerie advertising on a regular basis. Visit or call retail lingerie shops, ask the salesperson what sells the most—item, style, color, size— and what trends are changing. They probably won't suspect you as being one of their competition and will freely give you as much information as they can.

Measure from one catalog or brochure to the next which products are promoted more, promoted less, discontinued, or introduced. Each page of advertising material is like shelf space in a lingerie shop—there's a limited supply of space that needs to produce the highest amount of profit—(see Producing Your Catalog for more info on your own space planning).

Compare one lingerie company to another. The items that are common to each and occupy the most space are definitely going to be the better sellers. You now can start seeing which products you might want to start with to guarantee your initial success.

Look at prices relative to the sample chart in the last section. Are prices higher, lower, the same? Just because a product has a higher price doesn't necessarily mean it cost more from the supplier. Each mail order lingerie company exercises its right to charge as much as they want for any of the items it sees fit.

Testing the Waters

You've seen what the competition is doing, but how will buyers respond to you and your products? You will be another unique lingerie mail order company that will provide products differently from your competition. How will your approach differ?

Testing the response of various items (style, color, size of photo and especially price) through your advertising (be it catalog, classified ad, display ad or other) will supply you with prime indicators of what options work better than others and what directions you need to go.

For example, say you place a classified ad for a single item (designer lace pantyhose, for instance) in a newspaper with a guaranteed circulation of 20,000 readers, at a price of $9.95 a pair. You get 75 paid replies, grossing $746.25 dollars. The following week, you place another ad for the same pantyhose but priced at $4.95. This time you receive 125 paid orders grossing $618.75. What does this tell you?

You sold far fewer pairs of pantyhose at $9.95 yet you grossed substantially more money. This is called price testing—changing the price of a given item and measuring the response each price generates. This may seem like a trick but it's not; buyers respond very differently to prices (and colors, looks, wording and trends) set at varying levels. Almost your entire business will be based on this simple act of testing—finding which combinations work best for you.

Testing for Buyers

Who wants lingerie? As we've shown before, almost everybody does, but you aren't going to send a mailer or brochure to everyone. You need to find the best target audiences that will respond to your products the most. Locating list brokers in your area and finding appropriate mailing lists of prospective buyers isn't that hard. Many list brokers have names that were compiled for other clothing or related item clients and can be provided to you. Like suppliers, shop around for the best deals and the most varieties. Explain the type of person you're trying to reach (sex, age, buying patterns, etc); almost all list brokers have their lists available by these categories.

Again, testing will be key for each selection of people you send advertising to. Some mailing lists will produce buyers that primarily want bras; others lists might produce a large selection of garter belts. On the whole, there will be a measurable response that will give you the information you're looking for.

How do you know which buyers are ordering from which lists or ads? Attaching a key code to each mailing you do, marking that particular mailing list flyer or display ad with a code or number that the buyer sends back with the order or will give over the phone will allow you to track which segment responds best. This is important to watch and measure to ensure that your promotion continues to go to the people who are actually buying your products.

A Different Approach

You might find that you don't have the proper amount of capital to start a full-fledged mail order lingerie business, but still want to participate in some capacity.

Many lingerie wholesalers have set up programs in which they supply you with all the needed materials—catalogs with your name printed on them, order forms, business cards—getting you started as an independent agent selling their products. This can be a much lower-cost way to get into the industry and find out all that you can.

Shirley of Hollywood, for example, can supply you with all the needed start-up information, advertising and product support to sell their products. They have wonderful full color catalogs, covering a range of styles and sizes, plus good wholesale prices and instructions on how to succeed as a lingerie marketer.

By getting involved as a seller for a wholesaler or manufacturer in this fashion, you must abide by their instructions and procedures on how you can advertise, find new clients and what territories you can cover. This will limit the amount of decision making and test marketing you can do—some suppliers restrict you to following their own routines—but will give you some very good experience should you decide to eventually start your own lingerie concern.

The Right Step

Whichever way you decide to approach the marketing aspects of your mail order lingerie business, always remember to test what you do and measure and compare results. This will be the greatest advantage you'll have over most of the competition and keep your business aware of the public's buying changes, trends and tastes.

My Marketing List of Potential Customers

_____

_____

_____

_____

_____

_____

_____

_____

_____

_____

_____

_____

_____

_____

_____

_____

_____

_____

_____

_____

_____

_____

_____

_____

Marketing: in General

Now that you have selected the kind of business you want to own, it is important to explore the need for it. A process called marketing research will provide you with the information you need to develop your business, plan methods of distribution or promotion, and set prices which are tailored to the audience you hope to attract.

In addition, your marketing research will provide you with information that will help when you are making decisions about a location, hours of operation, the specific types of services and/or products to sell and how to gear your advertising.

Identifying Your Market

The process of identifying your audience may seem to be an extremely complex process, however, you can develop a perfectly workable and valuable marketing report using the guidelines that follow and adapting them to your particular situation. Basically, there are five factors used to target the market:

Population: The number of households in the region you are considering as a target for your business is crucial as you must have a sufficient population base to produce the sales you need to generate a profit. Equally important is the circulation and age range of readers of any magazine you will be focusing your advertising on for specific products. If, for example, the readership of a particular publication is largely of retirement age, it does not fare well if you are planning to sell products for infants. It would, however, work in your favor if you are promoting health products or even gift items.

Income: Your potential customers must have the income to purchase goods and services. Consumers in the 35-65 age group generally have considerable income, which they spend on household items, personal grooming and sporting goods. This is not to discount the over-65 age group, a good-size and growing segment of the nation's population that, depending on the region, will have adequate discretionary income (money after taxes and necessities) to spend, or the 18-35 age group, which is a desirable market for clothing, personal and recreational items.

Competition: The recent influx of frozen yogurt shops in warm climate regions made it difficult for late-comers to make a dent in the market. This is almost always the case and, therefore, competition shouldn't be a negative factor. Rather, it should spur you on to stretch your creativity by coming up with something brand new or a similar product or service that is superior to those being offered by the competition—either through quality, selection or price.

Product or service market match: Basically, this means that you must be able to attract those consumers whom you have the resources to serve. As an example, if your idea of the perfect business involves national distribution of your patented weight-training equipment, you must: (a) reach an audience that is receptive and interested in body building through a carefully designed advertising campaign and (b) have the financing available to supply and ship the product.

Desire: Your objective is to match your product or service to the needs and desires of a particular group of consumers who will be responsive. It is often difficult to figure out exactly what your target market wants; however, through observation of what the competition is doing, it should be possible to recognize a need.

Market Research Techniques

Large corporations often have in-house marketing staffs that conduct extensive research on a continuing basis to ensure that the products or services being offered are in line with the marketplace.

Obviously, this is an expensive and time-consuming process—one that you undoubtedly want to avoid.

Through several easy and inexpensive methods, you can find out everything you want to know about your potential market. The first step, however, is to determine exactly what information you need. It might be trends in population figures or regional economy or how many new homes were built within the last five years in your area.

The nearest Census Bureau office and your local chamber of commerce are consistently good sources for regional statistics. The reference librarian at the public library can steer you toward other local data and fact sheets that will give you the specifics you seek. Also, the Small Business Administration compiles extensive marketing information, in addition to material on operating procedures for specific types of businesses.

Check the Directory of Trade Associations at the library to find the name and address of the advisory board for your industries (or check the Resources listed at the end of this Guide). These trade boards exist to provide associates with marketing statistics, management tips and a wealth of valuable information. Often it only takes a phone call to get more details than you could ever use.

Another excellent source of information on population, income and sales figures is the annual survey of buying power published by Sales and Marketing Management Magazine, which breaks the information down by county and cities in the United States and should be available through the library.

Media Kits and Personal Contact

The advertising departments of local magazines and newspapers undoubtedly have a "Media Kit" available for potential advertisers, which they will gladly send you upon request. These packets contain a breakdown of their advertising rates and specifications, a description of why advertising with them is to your benefit and, most important, a profile of their readership. A friendly conversation with one of their salespeople should give you a wealth of data.

Talking with the people you will be buying supplies, equipment and products from is another excellent source. They can give you a good rundown on trends, as well as an overview of current sales figures for their products. Since they are hoping you will eventually use them as a supplier for your business, they will be more than happy to give you free information.

> ## Five Factors Used in Targeting Your Market
>
> 1. Population
> 2. Income
> 3. Competition
> 4. Market Match
> 5. Desire

It is, of course, often possible to gauge what the competition is doing and to glean information from them. There are two approaches when talking to people who are soon to be in direct competition. One is to be up-front and honest about your business plans and appeal to their sense of "industry spirit."

Surprisingly, you will find the direct approach works in the majority of cases as most people are genuinely interested in and supportive of others trying to make it in their field. It is better for everyone if "industry" standards are maintained and competitors have a healthy rapport. And, except in extreme situations such as a very small community, there is generally enough business to go around. It shouldn't be difficult to capture your share of the market, especially if you can develop something unique to attract them.

On the other hand, if competitors are less than receptive, it may be necessary to partake in a bit of super-sleuthing to get the information you want. A little brainstorming with friends should result in a few good ideas if you find it necessary to resort to investigative techniques.

Focus Groups

If you really want to go into depth with your marketing study, you might consider gathering together a group of people (family members, a social or church group, or friends) for a "focus" session to determine whether your product or service will match the needs of the prospective audience. This involves presenting your proposed business idea, with product samples if applicable, and creating a questionnaire that calls for specific answers from the group members.

This method is often used by major companies when they are testing new products and, in fact, there are private companies around the nation who do nothing but put focus groups together and set up testing sites in stores, shopping malls and street corners to obtain spontaneous and objective input from potential consumers.

The questions you would want to include on your questionnaire would ideally cover such aspects as how often members of the focus group have used a similar service or product in the past, what they liked about it, what they found to be unsatisfactory, how they feel it could have been improved, whether they would be willing to try another, their age, income and any specifics that relate to your proposed business.

For mail order lingerie, the questions might include a

breakdown of the top three reasons people in your focus group would consider using a service like yours, what type of lingerie items they would purchase and what additional services they would like to see offered. This kind of information will give you an immediate edge on the competition when you are ready to start advertising.

Analyzing Your Research

The bottom line in conducting your research is that you want to zero in on information that provides insights on the potential for your business idea before you invest time, money and energy in setting it up.

> *The greatest thing in the world is not so much where we stand as in what direction we are moving.*
>
> *Oliver Wendell Holmes*

If, for example, you were considering starting your business in a small community and your focus group information indicated that only 10 percent of the local residents would consider using it, you would definitely want to reconsider the validity of your concept or figure ways to promote it on a broader scale. On the other hand, if your marketing research pointed out that 90 percent of the population thought it was the greatest idea since sliced bread and that 50 percent would have an immediate need for it, the potential for your business would be much greater and proceeding with the idea would probably guarantee a profitable venture.

Buy an inexpensive notebook to help you keep track of your marketing data. Use a separate page for each category you are researching. The notebook will serve as your personal, ongoing market study to be reviewed and amended as your business grows and the audience you are serving changes.

Plan to update your information as new studies are published (generally an annual event) indicating changes in population, economy or buying and spending trends. Most newspapers publish synopses of local, state and federal studies of this nature, so maintaining your notebook shouldn't be a problem. You should also reserve several pages to record comments and suggestions from customers once your business is established, which will help you personalize the service to the market and keep you a step ahead of your competitors.

Spend as much time as needed to feel comfortable about your marketing project.

The important point is that the results of your research are comprehensive enough to provide you with concrete information on who your potential customers are and how you can best reach them.

Target audience:

_____

_____

_____

_____

Ideas for reaching the audience:

_____

_____

_____

_____

_____

_____

_____

_____

_____

Additional research information:

_____

_____

_____

_____

_____

Review

- I have completed my entrepreneurial profile to determine my strengths and weaknesses. ⎯⎯⎯⎯⎯

- My friends and/or relatives have given me additional input based on the profile. ⎯⎯⎯⎯⎯

- I am aware of the advantages and disadvantages of going into business for myself. ⎯⎯⎯⎯⎯

- Time is not a problem; I can easily devote the time I'll need to build my business. ⎯⎯⎯⎯⎯

- The important people in my life are supportive of my decision. ⎯⎯⎯⎯⎯

- I have analyzed my personal cash flow to insure that I can support myself and my family for at least six months or until the business is solvent. ⎯⎯⎯⎯⎯

- I feel confident about my future as a business owner at this point. ⎯⎯⎯⎯⎯

- I know what people want as far as my business is concerned. ⎯⎯⎯⎯⎯

- I have conducted informal studies to determine my potential customers and understand their needs. ⎯⎯⎯⎯⎯

- I have analyzed the competition, know what they offer and have a general idea about their success ratio. ⎯⎯⎯⎯⎯

- I have done my marketing research and know how to get in touch with the audience I want to reach. _____

- I have contacted the trade association for my industry and have accumulated facts and figures regarding the pros and cons of starting my own business. _____

- I feel confident that my product or service is saleable. _____

5

Location: Home or Commercial Office?

Mail order lingerie could be an ideal enterprise to start from home. However, whether you'll be permitted to operate such a business from your home will depend on local zoning ordinances, perhaps your landlord, or other restrictions. Laws pertaining to the operation of home businesses vary by county and state. It's illegal to conduct a home-based business in certain counties, while in many others across the country it's acceptable as long as local requirements are met.

The Home Office

By operating all aspects of your mail order lingerie business from home, you'll save much-needed capital that would otherwise be spent on a commercial location. That money could go toward your all-important early-stage marketing.

If you live alone, you can basically set up your business anywhere that is comfortable for you. But if you share your living quarters with other people, it may be necessary to use a little creativity in planning an office area in a home-based business situation. A spare room, a basement or attic or family room can be turned into an office quite simply with the addition of a worktable or desk, shelving for storage and a telephone.

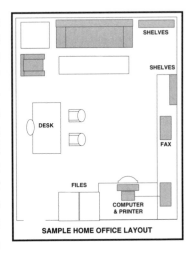

The main consideration, once you get the business rolling, is to have a permanent base of operations so that you can leave unfinished work without disturbance and that you have a place to put supplies and business records for easy access. Do not, under any circumstances, attempt to do bookkeeping and other functions at the kitchen table or on a folding card table. You will find yourself spending countless hours having to put things away or move them somewhere else to accommodate family life.

Utilities and Phone

The home-based business has an additional advantage: Your phone line and utilities are already in place. Any additional equipment is easy to obtain from your utility carriers because you already have an established payment history.

Single-line telephone systems are adequate for most small businesses. But if your business eventually outgrows a single-line system, you'll need a multi-line system enabling you to accept several calls simultaneously and switch between lines.

Regardless of whether you need a single line or a multi-line system, some basic options are now available when choosing equipment.

Programmable memory allows automatic storage and instant dialing of phone numbers by pressing a button or entering a code.

Automatic redial reconnects the last number dialed, in some cases redialing at specific intervals until the call goes through.

Speed dialing allows you to quickly access frequently dialed numbers by using a one- to four-digit code.

Call waiting is especially useful for businesses with single lines, allowing you to take incoming calls while putting the original caller on hold.

Conference calling is often a related feature of call waiting, allowing you to simultaneously speak with two or more parties at multiple locations.

Call forwarding routes incoming calls to a preprogrammed phone number at another location.

Cordless phones are especially useful for the home business, allowing you to make or accept calls from any location in the house. Because cordless phones vary in quality, it's recommended that you thoroughly research the market before buying.

Speaker phones allow you to carry on conversations without the constraint of holding a receiver. One of the main benefits is that you can accomplish other tasks while waiting on hold. They're also useful for note-taking and similar chores during business conversations.

Voice mail is a combination answering, routing, and messaging system that can help cut front-office payroll costs while maximizing efficiency. Customers dialing a voice mail number are greeted by a recorded message and given a menu of options: direct-dialing employees in other departments; leaving messages for one or more individuals; receiving additional recorded information; and using the voice mail system with a rotary-dial phone.

The cost of voice mail has been scaled down dramatically in recent years, and is now available for small or even one-person businesses, presenting a first-class image while actually saving you money (not only in payroll costs but in avoiding potential lost revenues from unanswered or misdirected calls).

Long-Distance Carriers

Whether you're a one-person home-based operation or an expanding business in a commercial location, long-distance service is, of course, essential.

With AT&T, U.S. Sprint, MCI, and a host of other carriers competing for your long-distance dollar, conflicting claims and a wide range of advertised services can leave the small-business person bewildered when trying to make a choice.

> *When deciding on a long-distance carrier, consider the areas of the country and the world you'll most frequently be calling and the monthly amount you plan to spend.*

The maze of carriers is actually two-tiered, the upper tier consisting of the major-network providers (such as AT&T) that offer direct lines to customers, and the lower tier made up of regional and national carriers that lease their lines from the major providers.

When deciding which carrier to use for your business, consider the following: the areas of the country and the world that you will most frequently be calling; the monthly amount you anticipate spending on long-distance calls;

the time of day you'll be making most of your calls; any seasonal calling patterns; and whether you'll be dealing only with clients statewide (in which case a regional WATS line would be a cost-effective choice).

In addition, read the various carriers' promotional information carefully. Does the carrier you're considering charge start-up or installation fees, or a flat monthly fee? If the latter, will you meet the carriers' minimum usage requirements, and are the services offered worth the monthly charge?

Other factors to consider include available volume discounts based on usage and dedicated lines giving you exclusive access to a telecommunications network.

800 Numbers

Businesses that market products and services regionally or nationally have found the 800 number among their most effective marketing tools. Customers who might not otherwise pay for a call cross-country now pick up the phone without hesitation—and frequently wind up requesting further information or making hefty credit card purchases.

Though 800 numbers can pay for themselves thousands of times over, the installation fees, service charges, and usage fees can be expensive. Consider carefully whether the potential costs outweigh the benefits. An alternative is the localized 800 number, available for small, highly targeted geographic areas. Consult your phone company for further information.

Guidelines for Commercial Locations

Once volume expands to the point that operating your business from home is no longer practical, you may need to move to a commercial location.

Selecting the right location is vital to the success of your business. The first factors you must analyze when looking for a commercial location are: (1) the community you want to live and/or work in, based on family needs, finances, your preference for a particular area because of health reasons or the fact that you have an established reputation in a certain area; and (2) the locations available within that community.

These factors are inter-related. You may want to settle down in an area with a limited number of suitable business locations available. Or you may have run across a number of viable sites in several communities or areas, in which case an investigation of each must be conducted, covering each of the points listed below:

a) *The type of business you are planning to operate.* Retail, wholesale and service businesses have slightly different requirements as determined by the type of products or service being offered and the market potential in a specific area.

b) *The demographics of the area.* This includes the number of consumers who want or need your product or service and are willing and able to pay your price; the median income and employment opportunities; age ranges of the major population group; and the volume of retail trade and projected expansion data. This information is available from census reports and chamber of commerce business reports accumulated during your market research project.

c) *Competition.* You must determine how many other similar establishments are serving the market and how their businesses are going to decide if there is room for your new venture. The best way to do this is by compiling a list of businesses from the phone book that you feel will be in direct competition and, if applicable, visiting their locations at different times of day to observe the activity levels. You might also talk with employees, who should be willing to answer your questions if you approach them in a friendly way. Often, the same kind of research can be accomplished effectively on the telephone.

d) *Traffic patterns.* Is your proposed location close to freeways, major intersections and/or a central business district? Is there sufficient parking? Is the foot traffic past the location strong and steady enough to guarantee walk-in trade, if needed to generate sales and profits? The ease with which customers can get to your location is a major consideration in terms of success.

e) *Your image.* Decide on the image you want to project, such as top quality products, superior service, low prices, convenience, before you go scouting for locations.

f) *The product or service.* If, for example, you were planning to sell high-priced, state-of-the-art European electronic equipment, it would be advisable to locate your business in a mall or on the main street of an economically comfortable community to ensure getting the response you need to survive. Generally, there are specific areas within a marketplace that cater to consumers in specific income levels and/or occupational groups, i.e., executives, blue collar workers, students, etc. Consider your product/service and the projected number of potential buyers within the community.

g) *The amount of rent required.* Locations having the highest potential of profit through consumer traffic (busy downtown areas, shopping malls, corner shops or stores with good frontage) are more expensive because competition keeps rents up to the maximum. The trade-off, however, is an increase in sales and, generally, a lower advertising budget because of the visibility factor.

As a new business owner, you may find that your allotted capital for rent is limited. Understanding and exploring the factors involved in selecting a location will help you find the best one for your money.

Retail Businesses

The guidelines indicated above are applicable for retail businesses. Poor location is one of the chief causes of failure among retail stores, but, on the other hand, the right location can be all it takes for even a mediocre business to thrive and grow.

Service Businesses

When clients are going to be visiting your place of business, the same principles of location selection apply as are indicated for retail. If clients will not be visiting, location selection can be based on rent, the amount of space needed and the convenience to you.

Wholesale or Manufacturing Businesses

Where you locate a wholesale business depends on your market. If dealing primarily with local retailers or customers, your location should be within easy driving distance of your clientele.

However, if most of your business is conducted through the mail or delivery services, you can base your selection on the best rent available and the convenience factor for you and your staff. When choosing a location for your wholesale business, warehousing needs are a vital consideration, as is projected expansion.

Before Signing a Lease

Unless you're planning to purchase the commercial location, rent your location from a family member or accept a temporary agreement in a location that is for sale, you will be required to sign a lease before moving in.

The most desirable agreement for you as a new business owner is a one-to-two year lease with a renewal option at a guaranteed rate for rent increases over a five to ten year period.

Rent for a commercial location is established either on a flat rate or a percentage basis. Under the flat rate, rent is generally based on the square footage of the shop and on the location or, in some cases, on potential volume. The percentage base involves a base amount of rent plus a pre-arranged percentage of monthly sales.

Your lease will also cover a number of other points, such as the liabilities and responsibilities of the landlord and of you, the tenant; i.e., who is to pay for specific repairs, renovations, tax increases and utilities, etc.

The lease may contain stipulations about the size of the exterior sign you can erect, hours of operation, insurance coverage and assignation of the lease to another party (a sublease).

Before signing a lease to set up your business, make sure that electrical lines are adequate enough to handle high volume usage, that you have restrooms for employees and/or clients, and convenient parking areas. Also check with the leasing agent to be certain you can make leasehold improvements (i.e., storage shelves, air conditioning, lighting) as the business warrants it.

It is recommended that you have an attorney review the lease carefully before you sign it to ensure that you understand all of the clauses and to serve as a negotiator, if necessary.

A Closet-Based Business

The very nature of mail order lends itself to being a home-based operation. The deciding factor for how much space your business will need depends on your own organization and inventory needs. If you are well organized, your business can be run quite efficiently from a single desk, with a computer and printer, phone and filing cabinet close by.

Since most of the office/management/planning portions of your business can be performed on a small desktop computer, your main concern for space needs will be for paper backup, catalogs, orders and shipping forms/invoices. A well organized filing cabinet or two should be able to handle these start-up necessities with enough room for the first year's growth.

On the inventory/fulfillment side of the business, you may want to consider how much product you'll be stocking and calculate the amount of space you'll require. Lingerie especially stands out in this area because of the small size of most of the products and the light weight of the materials. If you were selling office furniture through the mail, you would need no less than a major warehouse—but you can fit a lot of bras and panties in an area no bigger than a garage.

One lingerie company owner we spoke to uses the "shoebox" technique for organizing and calculating how much product she orders each month. She keeps two closets in her house and a rack of shelving in the garage filled with 9" x 15" x 5" shoeboxes marked for each item she sells. She knows that she can fit 50 panties in a standard shoebox or 25 bras or 15 camisoles and so on. The total amount of space she allots for home inventory is equal to 280 shoeboxes. Luckily, over time she was able to accumulate all the shoeboxes at no charge (her sister-in-law owns a shoe store, in case you're wondering).

Each box is labeled for style, sizes and colors, and as you can see, she's able to keep a fairly sizable inventory on hand (almost 4,700 panties alone!). She limits her inventory to the "top sellers" and uses her wholesaler to dropship for orders that request exotic products, expensive items or special sizes. (See the Operations section for more on Inventory Control and Planning.)

Ideally, converting a spare bedroom or guest room into a home office should accommodate a mail order lingerie business very well. If possible, utilizing garage space for inventory and shipping supplies will free up needed room for expansion in the house when the business starts growing.

If the business really starts booming, look to renting a storage facility nearby for inventory or rent a warehouse with office space to run the entire operation. This will increase expenses, but when the business gets too large to operate efficiently at home, you should be making enough money to justify the costs.

Just remember that no matter where you decide to operate your mail order lingerie business, from a New York high-rise to an Oregon basement, your real concern is the legitimate appearance that should accompany all outgoing packages, catalogs, and correspondence. Since your only contact with the "outside world" will be through these items, having good looking packaging and promotional material will give the impression of a large, professional and caring company. The only difference being that, as a home-based mail order business, you're a small, professional and caring company.

If setting up my business at home, I have:

- Checked with the city and county offices in my area regarding required licenses and permits and zoning regulations for home-as-office. _____
- Set aside a room or an area in my home that will be used exclusively for my business. _____
- Had a separate telephone installed and have purchased an answering machine or contracted with a message service. _____
- Set up a separate business bank account. _____
- Informed friends and family of my business routine and specific working hours to reduce interruptions and distractions. _____

If setting up in a commercial location, I have:

- Investigated rental rates for the area I am interested in. _____
- Checked traffic flow, parking and foot-traffic around my proposed location. _____
- Determined that my business is compatible with others in the area. _____
- Talked with my prospective landlord about improvements, maintenance and rent increases. _____
- Had my lawyer check the rental agreement and any local zoning regulations. _____
- Checked prices on storage units, work tables or shelves. _____
- Planned a layout that I feel will work well for the location and my storage, display and office needs. _____

6

SETTING UP YOUR BUSINESS
AT HOME

There is a lot of appeal in operating your business from home.

Thousands of successful businesses have been started in a basement, a spare room or on the kitchen table. Henry Ford, for example, founded the Ford Motor Company in his garage and Jean Nidetch started Weight Watchers in her living room as a support group for friends who wanted to lose extra pounds. Both of these businesses, and many more like them, became successful multi-million-dollar corporations, despite humble beginnings.

The Small Business Administration estimates that there are close to 10 million home-based businesses in the United States today and, of these, more than 30% are owned and operated by women. These figures have been substantiated by an AT&T study, as well as by the U.S. Department of Labor.

Starting a home-based business has provided an

opportunity for many people, who might otherwise never have the chance, to become entrepreneurs. Women, especially, have discovered that they can build a profitable, satisfying business at home while still being available for their families.

For others, a home-based business is the ticket out of the world of the urban commuter. In fact, a home-based business is the perfect way to try something new to see how it works while still working another job to pay the bills. Once the business has proven itself and is realizing a profit, you can leave the job to devote full time to your new venture.

Couples often find that investing time and energy in building a business together at home develops stronger relationships in addition to increasing joint income. For the retired and for those with minor physical disabilities, it is a path to staying involved, exploring self-sufficiency and guaranteeing a profitable future.

The Advantages of Establishing a Home-Based Business

- Ability to start your business immediately
- Minimal start-up capital needed
- No rent or excessive set-up charges for utilities required
- Comfortable working conditions
- Reduced wardrobe expenses
- No commuting
- Tax benefits
- Elimination of office politics
- Flexibility and independence
- Full utilization and recognition of skills
- Low risk for trial and error

Start-Ups Never Change

As with any new business, whether located at home or in a commercial location, it is important to follow the basic guidelines for start-up, including: conducting a market survey, drawing up a business plan, setting goals, reviewing capital needs and projected income, developing an advertising campaign and establishing a professional image.

A mail order lingerie business is, of course, tailored to the home, offering a number of advantages for the business owner who is just starting out.

Setting up your business at home automatically eliminates up to 75% of the start-up costs and responsibilities required for an office or storefront operation. You are, in your home, already making rent or mortgage payments and paying for your own telephone service, insurance and utilities.

In many instances, a commercial location will require $10,000 just to open the doors with basic leasehold improvements and/or equipment. In addition, valuable time and energy is saved in scouting for the location, having utilities installed and decorating the premises.

Getting Your Feet Wet

A home-based business gives you the opportunity to test the waters with a minimum of risk. This is especially beneficial to first time entrepreneurs, who may prefer to learn and grow with the business in the comfort of their home without the pressures that operating out of a commercial location often brings.

As a hedge against inflation, the home-based business is a natural. In addition to low start-up, tax deductions (for use of your home as an office and your business expenses) provide relief from a seemingly endless outflow of cash on mortgage or rent payments. You must, however, be aware of the tax laws, which allow deductions only for that part of the home "used exclusively and regularly" for business and, as of last year, limited to a modified net income of the business.

After the business is running smoothly, you will find

that the potential to earn money is greater because of reduced overhead. Your production will increase because you have more control over your schedule and fewer of the typical interruptions that arise in a commercial setting. Generally, home-based entrepreneurs claim that an added benefit is reduced stress, despite the fact that they are working long hours.

Of course, as with any business arrangement, there are also disadvantages to setting up your business in your home. By recognizing them, however, it is possible to address and minimize the problems before they come up.

Getting to Work

One of the biggest problems faced by home-based entrepreneurs is being able to establish a productive work schedule. There are different types of interruptions that come up in a home environment, including visits from friends and neighbors, household chores that need to be done, the temptation of television and the daily paper when there is work to be produced. There is also no one around to spur you on.

A helpful suggestion for getting down to work is to dress in the morning as if you were going out to a regular job. This alone will help you set your priorities for the day.

The best solution, however, is to establish regular working hours from the onset (although you do have the flexibility as a home-based business owner to arrange your schedule around the times you know you are the most productive). If friends want to visit, politely explain to them that you are operating a business that requires your full concentration and arrange a suitable time to get together according to your schedule.

It is also important, if you have family, that they are supportive and willing to arrange their lives as much as possible around your schedule. This can be dealt with through frequent family discussions about what you are doing and how the business operates.

Another difficult area is learning to separate business and pleasure. A home-based business often makes it very easy to work day and night on a project. Again, it is important to allot time for personal activities. The secret to remember is that the work will get done much more efficiently if you are relaxed and rested.

It's also a good idea to have the business set up in a separate room or area that can be shut off from your personal living space after working hours. This will more easily enable you to separate work from leisure time.

Home-based business owners often experience feelings of isolation from those in their industry.

One way to eliminate this is to join local groups, such as the chamber of commerce and networking groups, and to, at least, attend the meetings. Check to see how many members are entrepreneurs, which will give you a built-in support system. By making yourself available to serve on committees, you'll be able to reach into the community and publicize your business for the cost of your involvement.

The Disadvantages of Establishing a Home-Based Business

- Success is based 100% on your efforts
- Difficult to establish solid work habits
- Difficult to know how to set competitive rates
- Limited support system
- Isolation
- Limited work space
- Disruption of personal life
- Clients are uncomfortable coming to your home
- Zoning restrictions

Reviewing Local Laws

Before getting started, it is important to check that zoning ordinances in your area will allow you to use your home for business purposes. Since zoning ordinances vary from city to city and county to county, it is necessary to contact the Planning Department of your regional government offices or talk with your attorney to find out what is allowed. Regulations are based on the type of business, the area to be used within your home, noise control, tax regulations, business signs and other aspects. You may also need a special permit or license.

If you are expecting clients to visit your home for business, it is best to have a separate room set up as an office so that when they come to discuss a purchase, they won't feel as if they are intruding on a family. If, however, an office is out of the question, make sure you arrange meetings during times when the family is away from home to ensure that there will be no interruptions.

> *God gives every bird its food, but he does not throw it in the nest.*
>
> *J. G. Holland*

Another option is to go to the client's location when you must have meetings or to offer pick-up and delivery service, if applicable. Depending on the business, however, and the quality of your work, client discomfort shouldn't be a major problem, according to a number of home-based business owners we have interviewed.

As an example, the number of home-based typesetting services has increased dramatically over the past few years, and we have never heard of any complaints or problems in this area. The bottom line, as far as the customer is concerned is still—and will always be—reliable service or high quality products and the knowledge that he or she is dealing with a professional.

The benefits of a home-based business to the beginning entrepreneur can mean the difference between working for someone else or turning a dream into reality.

The key element, as with any business, is motivation, a needed product or service, careful planning and the desire to succeed. But sometimes, just knowing that the expenses of establishing a business in a commercial location are alleviated by setting up a home-based enterprise is enough to push you forward to success, one small step after another.

7

START-UP BASICS: FIGURING COSTS

Having decided that you are ready and able to accept the challenge of starting your own business, it is necessary to take a look at your overall financial picture. Even if you have a healthy savings account, or feel you can start your business with a minimal capital investment, diagnosing your personal financial situation will help you determine ongoing expenses.

The easiest way to estimate exactly how much money you will need to get your business started and to cover expenses, including personal living expenses, for the first six months is to prepare a Cost of Living or Cash Flow Statement and a Projected Expense Chart. Samples are provided on the following pages for your use.

Preparing the Projected Expense Chart will give you a fairly accurate picture of what it will cost to open the doors and indicate how much income you must generate to realize a profit. The other advantage of creating these charts early in the game is that when you do find that you want to explore funding options, you will already have two of the required documents prepared and will need only to update them.

Your first step is to ask yourself the following questions:

a) Do I generally pay my bills on time or wait until my creditors start sending me collection notices?

b) Have I regularly reconciled my bank statement so I know how much money I have in my checking account at any given time?

c) Is my philosophy "If I've got it, I spend it" or do I typically carefully plan how I am going to use my income?

d) Have I ever developed a personal budget so I know how much money is coming in, how much is going out and what I have left over?

These are important aspects of your financial personality that will be helpful to understand when running your business. As your business and subsequent involvement with financial matters grows, it will be vital that you have a handle on your philosophy about money. And there is no time like in the beginning, when your business concept is being formed, to start learning.

The Cash Flow Statement

Using the chart on page 76, you can determine your personal living expenses for the past three to six months to help you gauge what you will need to survive during the early stages of your business.

The easiest way to complete the statement is to use your checkbook register, if you write checks for most purchases, and/or cash receipts and copies of money orders as research tools. If your expenses are relatively consistent from month to month, you should be able to get an overview by analyzing one month. A more accurate picture will emerge if you break down income and expense for three to six months to account for periodic payments, such as taxes, insurance and seasonal spending.

Using the samples provided, fill in the amounts in each category from your checkbook register or receipts. Use a separate sheet for every month that you are analyzing. For miscellaneous spending, a standard calculation is 5% of monthly income. Add up each month's expenses, total them all and then divide that figure by the number of months you are analyzing. This will give you an average month expense figure.

Follow the same procedure for income. You can then subtract your expenses from your income to see where you stand. If you have computed your figures accurately, you might run across a few surprises. It isn't unusual to discover that we spend more money than we realize, often on miscellaneous, unneeded purchases. You may be able to see some areas where you can cut back.

The main point, however, is that you now know (a) how much or whether you can afford to invest your own money in your new business and (b) what it costs you to live comfortably, which will help you set income goals for the business.

Cash Flow Statement
Month of _____

Income		Expenses	
Wages	$_____	Rent or mortgage	$_____
Miscellaneous	$_____	Auto loan	$_____
		Gas & car repairs	$_____
		Auto insurance	$_____
TOTAL	$_____	Life insurance	$_____
		Medical insurance	$_____
		Homeowners insurance	$_____
		Taxes	$_____
Savings	$_____	Loan payments	$_____
		Food: At home	$_____
Credit Line	$_____	Food: Dining out	$_____
		Telephone	$_____
Home Equity	$_____	Utilities	$_____
		Household repairs, etc.	$_____
		Medical bills	$_____
		Credit card payments	$_____
		Interest expense	$_____
		Clothing/ dry cleaning	$_____
		Travel	$_____
		Miscellaneous	$_____
		Savings	$_____
		TOTAL	$_____

Start-up Costs

Every business owner has specific standards about how he or she wants to run his or her operation. One person may feel perfectly comfortable waiting until he or she is making a profit to order business cards. Another wouldn't dream of opening the doors without cards, brochures and letterhead already printed.

You will have your own ideas about what you need before opening your business. Then, you must find out what it will cost and, if at all possible, prepare the Start-up Statement as outlined in this section.

It is also advisable to figure how much it will cost to run the business for three to six months, using the sample Projected Expense Forecast that follows. A six month projection should give you the opportunity to start getting an idea of your profits down the line.

Preparing the Start-up Statement and Projected Expense Forecast involves conducting some research. For example, to estimate the cost of business cards or letterhead stationery, contact several printers or copy shops in your area and obtain quotes. Call the local newspaper for prices on different types of ads, including display and classified. An insurance agent will be able to give you an estimate on liability coverage. Check with the telephone company for information and rates on installing a phone line. You can also start to shop around to find the best prices on office supplies, equipment and materials needed to conduct business.

After completing your research, incorporate the information on the blank charts. Some of your figures, such as those for telephone expenses, will be "guesstimated." But the final figure will give you a good idea of start up and operational costs for the first six months.

Start-up Costs

Furniture: Purchase price $_____
            Down payment required $_____

Fixtures: Purchase price $_____
            Down payment required $_____

Equipment: Purchase price $_____
            Down payment required $_____

Installation and deliver costs $_____
Decorating & leasehold improvements $_____
Deposits: Utilities and rent $_____
Fees: Legal, accounting, consulting, etc. $_____
Licenses & permits $_____
Starting inventory $_____
Supplies $_____
Printing $_____
Pre-opening advertising & promotion $_____
Miscellaneous: $_____

Total Start-up Expense $_____

Less: Available Start-up Capital (minus) $_____

Total Amount Needed $_____

Have this sample chart enlarged at your local copy shop if planning to use it as part of your Business Plan. Enlarging it will cost you a few cents, but can save you many dollars in the long run, because of the increased awareness of your financial picture.

Projected Expense Statement

Months	1st	2nd	3rd	4th	5th	6th
Rent						
Utilities						
Telephone						
Insurance						
Professional Services						
Taxes & Licenses						
Advertising						
Office Supplies						
Office Equipment						
Inventory						
Business auto expense						
Travel expense						
Entertainment						
Dues & subscriptions						
Salaries						
Owner's draw						
Loan payments						
Interest payments						
Miscellaneous						
TOTALS						

Utilizing the same theory, you can develop a Projected Income Statement, drawing from industry figures available through your trade association or other research sources.

This would include all income realized from cash sales, collection on outstanding invoices, credit card sales and miscellaneous income. By subtracting your total expenses from total income, you will get a clear picture of projected profit or loss.

All of these statements will be requested by loan officers, venture capitalists and the Small Business Administration (SBA) if and when you apply for a loan.

They require this kind of paperwork to ensure that you have basic business knowledge and a commendable track record and are serious about your venture. You will also be required to fill out a personal financial statement, available through the lending institution, especially if you are the sole owner or a general partner in the business.

Start-up Expenses*

Low-End Start-up
(Home-Based Operation)

Start-up Marketing/Advertising	$3,500.00
Office Supplies/Equipment	2,000.00
Initial Inventory	1,500.00
Utilities	250.00
Insurance (monthly)	100.00
Licenses/Filing Fees	150.00
Total Investment	**$7,500.00**

Average Investment
(Larger Operation)

Office Furniture	600.00
Business Licenses/Consultation	200.00
Fictitious Name Statement (FNS)	15.00
Publishing FNS	30.00
Business Telephone Installation	1,500.00
Answering Machine	100.00
Fax Machine	300.00
Insurance (monthly)	200.00
Start-up Marketing	5,000.00
Inventory	10,000.00
Catalog Production	8,500.00
Total investment	**$26,445.00**

*These prices are general averages and will vary according to region.

8

BASIC REQUIREMENTS: EQUIPMENT AND SUPPLIES

Computer System

One of your basic needs will be a good word processor, enabling you to easily perform a wide variety of tasks from marketing to billing.

Computer prices are dropping rapidly, and you can currently buy a perfectly good used system for under $500; check the classifieds of local publications. If you wish to have the latest and greatest, expect to pay $1,500 to $3,000 for it. If you have the time to shop around, you can purchase a good computer system for between $700 and $1,500. Also, look for new-merchandise bargains at grand openings of computer stores, year-end closeouts, etc.

Frequently, the computer you purchase will come equipped with word processing and other proprietary software packages, so shop around for the best deal.

Software

There are a number of software packages well-suited to run a lingerie operation. However, you don't necessarily need an industry-specific software package, as long as the business software package you choose has the following: accounting; the ability to link to other software systems; word processing; report generation; and a graphics capability.

When choosing a software package, begin by analyzing all the essential elements: everything from data processing to accounting. Then contact computer stores and software manufacturers for information, brochures, etc. Make sure the software is compatible with your hardware if you already own a computer; otherwise, tailor the hardware to the best software package(s).

One alternative is to buy an integrated package combining several applications, from accounting to word processing and database management.

Arrange for a software demonstration, and bring along your list of requirements. If you're not computer-literate, bring along someone who is, and during the demonstration be sure to use the equipment yourself, making sure it's user-friendly.

Most important, compare each software system with your needs, not the features of other systems. You ultimately are the one who has to use the program and be satisfied with it. If it costs hundreds of dollars and has a lot of bells and whistles you'll never need or use, keep looking. Shop carefully and base your choice on your own business projections and the market you'll be serving. One alternative is to buy an integrated package—one combining several applications (word processing, accounting, database management, and so on).

The leading packages in all software categories are too numerous to outline here. What follows is a glance at the proven winners and most commonly used programs (most are available both for IBM-compatibles and Macintosh): spreadsheet/accounting (Lotus 1-2-3, Excel); database management (Paradox, dBASE, Quattro Pro); word processing (WordPerfect, Microsoft Word); graphics (CorelDraw!, QuickDraw); and integrated software (Microsoft Works is generally considered one of the best available).

Printers

Printers are broken down into three categories: laser (essential for high-quality graphic and desktop publishing applications), dot-matrix (still the biggest seller, and acceptable for a range of applications from correspondence to billing), and ink-jet (used for graphic and business applications).

Laser. Hewlett-Packard dominates much of the laser market with its LaserJet series. Ask your computer dealer for the lowest-cost LaserJet (at this writing Hewlett-Packard makes a good low-cost alternative perfect for the home office). Also consider low-cost offerings from Okidata.

Dot-matrix. Popular choices here include printers from Epson, Panasonic, Okidata, and Microline. If you don't have a need for high-quality graphic output and plan to use your computer for correspondence and accounts payable/receivable, dot-matrix printers are the low-cost way to go.

Ink jet. Again, the leader in this category is Hewlett-Packard with a popular DeskJet series that comes in both black-and-white and color models.

Modems

Modems transmit and receive computer data over telephone lines, connecting the home or office-based business with the outside world, from a print shop down the street to a client in Europe.

Modems usually are categorized by their transmission (or baud) rate, measured in bits (or characters) per second. Baud rates are typically 300, 1200, and 2400, but more commonly are upwards of 9600. Modems 1200 baud and higher are recommended for long documents. The higher the baud rate, the faster the transmission time and thus the lower your phone bill, since transmission time is billed in the same manner as a phone call. A recent addition to the modem family is the fax modem, turning your phone into an all-purpose retrieval/transmission center.

Notebooks

These lightweight, battery-powered laptops can be used as stand-alone systems or as add-ons to your home computer, in both cases providing system access at remote locations—from the back seat of a limo or a 747 at 30,000 feet. They're more costly than their more conventional counterparts (upwards of $2,500), but can be worth the expense if you frequently need computer access at a variety of locations.

CD-ROMs

The storage medium of the future has not only arrived, it's standard equipment on a number of computer systems, enabling users to store 150,000 pages of text per disc and take a massive load off their hard drives. CD-ROMs store everything from downloaded fonts to 60-million-word dictionaries, and represent the 21st century's ultimate interactive resource. They'll eventually replace conventional newspapers and libraries, becoming the central link in home information systems.

Fax Machines

Fax machines have become standard equipment in commercial offices and increasingly in the home office, allowing local or worldwide transmission of information in a matter of seconds.

Fax machines come in a variety of sizes, from affordable compact models (recommended for the small business) to larger floor-standing units. Some models are also combination answering machines and flatbed copiers. Some of the higher-end systems use laser printer technology well suited to graphics-oriented data.

Some of the smaller units are now available new for about $275 (shop carefully) and can be bought on the used market for considerably less. Leading manufacturers include Canon, Xerox, and Sharp.

Furniture and Supplies

You will need basic office furniture when expanding your business. Whenever possible buy used furniture. A desk for general marketing and billing is, of course, essential. But if you plan on computerizing, you'll also need a computer desk with room for a printer and modem. You'll also need shelving for computer disks, books, and other miscellaneous items.

Consider the benefits of a good calculator with tape for billing and record-keeping and shelves for storing a library of reference books and other relevant publications. You'll also need such standard supplies as card files, file cabinets, and staplers. In addition, you'll need letterhead stationery, business cards, printed envelopes, and brochures that explain your service.

All are available at local stationers and office supply

stores. For record-keeping, you'll need index cards, large manila envelopes, files, and invoice forms. Even with a computer storing a lot of your data, these items are still necessary.

Check for wholesale distributors in your area or ask other business people for good suppliers. Get estimates from two or three suppliers before making a final decision. Business supplies can be obtained from mail order companies as well.

Buy or Lease? Making the Choice

You can buy new or used equipment from dealers and independent sellers. Or, if you don't mind rummaging through other people's lives, you can find incredible bargains on supplies and equipment at garage sales, swap meets, thrift shops run by charitable organizations or auctions. Often, it is well worth the time involved because the savings can be tremendous.

Before investing money, do your homework. Talk with other business owners to find out which brand of equipment they use and why they prefer it over other choices on the market. This will help you make the best decision based on your needs and budget.

Also, talk with independent dealers who carry a broad line of similar types of equipment. They can give you insights on maintenance, longevity, service contracts and prices.

They will also be able to tell you when to expect a drop in price for the item you are interested in, although you can count on seeing sales on major equipment such as computers and other big-ticket items at store openings and during special sales.

Cash or Credit?

Unless you are planning to pay cash for an equipment purchase, you will either make a down payment and set up a payment schedule with the dealer or take out a loan with the bank. With interest rates for bank loans currently running at about 9-12%, you might be able to find a dealer who is willing to handle the financing at a lower rate.

Although this method is a less effective way of establishing creditworthiness, it will serve to get the business going. Another advantage is that if you should find yourself in a tight cash flow situation at any time, a private dealer/lender with whom you have a personal relationship is much more likely to be flexible . . . without charging you a penalty for late payment.

Buying Used Equipment

When buying used equipment from a dealer, the chances of it's being in working condition are generally pretty good. Dealers have a reputation to uphold and will stand behind their merchandise, especially if they are firmly established in the community. There are, however, several ways you can scout around to ensure that the one you decide to work with is reputable:

• Find a store with membership in the local chamber of commerce. Although this is not an iron clad guarantee, it does indicate the store ownership's interest in following business standards established within the community.

• If the dealer also sells new equipment, it is highly likely that much of the used equipment has been traded in by people who are upgrading. You may be able to get an excellent bargain on an item that has been well maintained by the former owner.

• If there is a service department on the premises, you

can be assured that used equipment has been reconditioned before being put on sale. It also increases your chances of getting fast, inexpensive and reliable service if needed at a later date.

• Used equipment dealers realize that it is not always easy to find a buyer and should be willing to work with you. Shopping around will give you an idea of average prices and will give you the information you need to negotiate. If the dealer won't work with you, keep looking.

• What are the terms of the warranty? Even used equipment should be covered for a short time for parts and labor, especially if it has been overhauled or reconditioned.

• Is the dealer willing to agree to offer a trade-in allowance on the item you are buying when you decide to upgrade? Of course, there will be stipulations based on wear and tear and time; however, he or she should be willing to consider it.

Buyer Beware

There are other ways to find and buy used equipment, but it falls into the realm of "Buyer Beware." If you choose to deal with private parties through the classified ads or with auctioneers selling off the inventory of a bankrupt business, you must be willing to take a chance. Although the prices will be easy on your budget, the cost of repairing a malfunctioning machine could result in a long-term drain on your profits.

> *The greatest inspiration is a challenge to attempt the impossible.*
>
> *A. Michelson*

This is not to say that there aren't bargains out there. In many cases, you will stumble across an incredible deal on a "like-new" computer, as an example. The secret is to know what you are looking for and to have a good idea of how it should work. Do your research by visiting with reliable used equipment dealers before you start looking.

When talking with a private parties, ask them how long they have owned the equipment, why they are selling it and if they have kept any repair bills that you can see. Trust your intuition in this kind of situation; if the person seems truly interested in providing you with as much information as possible, chances are the equipment is everything they say it is or isn't. If they tell you it needs a new part, for example, find out what the replacement part costs and ask if they would deduct it from the selling price.

When you go to see the equipment, make sure it runs. Test it out if possible, measure it to make sure it will fit into the space you have available and decide whether you can move it yourself or will have to arrange transportation. Before buying it, try to find out whether there is a servicing outlet nearby or if you must send away for parts, which can be time-consuming and costly, especially when it comes to older models. Occasionally you will run across an individual who is making payments on a piece of equipment still under warranty. This can be a great deal for you since he or she will probably accept a small amount

> ### Referral Discounts
>
> *Here's a way to boost your income that will make your clients happy to promote the business.*
> *Offer clients who provide you with the name of a potential listing (or who have someone call you) a discount on billing. If it results in a job, give a 10% discount to the referring party.*

of cash and let you take over the payments. Be sure to transfer ownership in writing to prevent complications if you need service under the warranty.

Auctions

Auctions are an excellent way to get good bargains. Watch the business and classified sections of the newspaper for ads about upcoming auctions. The ad will include dates, the reason for the auction (liquidation or bankruptcy), location, time and a partial list of items. In most cases, there will be a preview, enabling potential buyers to view the merchandise before the bidding begins.

By all means, take advantage of the preview to inspect and select equipment you want to bid on. A fee will be required for a bidder registration number, which is held up when you make a bid so the auctioneer's spotters know who has purchased a particular item.

The two rules to remember at auctions are: (a) cash or a personal check for the full purchase amount must be paid on the day of the auction and (b) don't move your hands or make significant gestures during bidding or you might find that you have purchased something you didn't want.

Leasing Equipment

Leasing is defined as a long-term agreement between two parties for the use of a specific item. The person who leases is known as the lessee, while the owner of the item is referred to as the lessor. Despite the fact that you do not own the equipment when you lease and so can not take advantage of depreciation on it for tax purposes, there are still many benefits for the beginning business owners.

Leasing lets you try out a piece of equipment for a given period of time to determine if it is the best product for your needs. Although you are locked into the terms of the lease, most lessors are flexible.

Know What You Need

Of course, the way to prevent this in the first place is to be absolutely clear about what you expect the equipment to do for you. The service representative from the leasing company is well versed in tailoring equipment to customer, so do not hesitate to ask questions about capabilities.

Most lessors offer good maintenance contracts, as they want to protect their equipment. Check to see what parts and/or labor are covered before signing the lease. The lessor should also be willing to provide technical advice at no charge, may be willing to offer installation and set-up of the equipment and also provide training, if required.

Payments can be arranged to fit your budgetary needs on a monthly, semi-annual or annual basis. This gives you the freedom to schedule payments for peak cash-flow periods. You can also negotiate the rates and length of time of the lease to keep monthly operating expenses at a minimum.

Conditional Sales Agreement

Under the provisions of a conditional sales agreement, you become the owner of the leased goods from the agreement date. At the end of the lease period, you are required to purchase the item for a pre-established price. This is often referred to as a balloon payment and should be agreed upon by you and the lessor prior to your signing the lease.

The conditional sales agreement, unlike most other leasing contracts, gives you the tax advantage of claiming depreciation on equipment. Depreciation refers to the decrease in the value of an asset because of wear and tear over a period of time.

You are entitled to deduct depreciation, based on value

when new, the estimated life of the item and the value at the end of that estimated life, from your income tax. It is best to work with your accountant on determining depreciation of fixed assets.

There is seldom a down payment, other than the first month's lease amount, required on a leased item, since leasing is generally 100% financed for the terms of the agreement. This frees your start-up or working capital for other uses.

True Lease Agreements

You can write off lease payments on your income tax, but only if you have a true lease contract. Under a true lease, the lessor owns the equipment at all times during the contract period. If you decided, at the end of the lease, that you wanted to buy the equipment, you would have to pay whatever purchase price was decided by the lessor.

Financial Lease

The financial lease covers a period that does not extend beyond the estimated life of the equipment. Payments must be made as stipulated on the date due and through to the end of the lease. It usually puts the responsibility and cost of maintenance on the lessee.

Operating Lease

The operating lease generally requires the lessor to handle maintenance of the equipment. It offers the option of cancelling the lease, but only if a cancellation clause has been included at the negotiating stage.

The most important aspects of leasing are the terms outlined in the formal lease. Have the lessor draw up a proposal for you, based on everything you have discussed in an initial meeting. If you have any trouble understanding the terms of the proposal, have your attorney review it with you. In fact, it is a definite advantage to have the final lease agreement checked by your attorney or accountant before you sign it.

What Your Lease Agreement Should Include

- The length of the contract in months or years.
- The rate you are to be charged, which is usually a percentage of the total purchase price computed on a monthly rate.
- Your payment schedule.
- Purchase option, if applicable, at the end of the lease.
- Renewal option, if applicable, which allows you to carry the lease over for an additional period of time.
- Cancellation agreement in the event you want or need to cancel the lease.
- Maintenance stipulations (who pays for parts & labor).
- Substitution options if updated equipment is introduced and you want to take advantage of improvements.
- Any provisions particular to the lease, including tax allowances for depreciation, insurance liability in case of loss or damage and your responsibilities in reporting a move or other major change.

Whether you decide to borrow, buy new equipment, find good used equipment or lease, be sure to get exactly what you need to keep costs at a minimum. This is especially important during the early stages of your business when cash is bound to be tight. You can always upgrade or add to your equipment inventory as profits increase.

9

SELECTING PROFESSIONALS

From the start-up stage and as your business continues to grow and prosper, you will need the assistance of several professionals, including a lawyer, an accountant and an insurance agent.

The best way to find a professional is, according to the majority of business owners, through personal recommendations from other entrepreneurs, especially those in similar businesses as yours, and from friends or relatives. The most important factor is that the person doing the recommending understands exactly what you will need from the professional you will be hiring.

For example, your cousin's divorce lawyer is probably not as well suited to helping you draw up a partnership agreement as the attorney a friend used to help them incorporate their business.

Before making a decision, talk to several recommended professionals until you find someone who can best satisfy your needs for the business as outlined below and who has a fee structure you can afford. Equally important is that it is someone whom you feel comfortable with, especially during those times when you are forced by external forces to call five times a week to resolve a problem or complete a specific task. In many cases, because attorneys and accountants often work on a particular business matter in conjunction with one another, the attorney you select may be able to suggest an accountant who can properly service your business, or vice versa.

If you are planning to hire an attorney or an accountant, you should start "interviewing" likely candidates eight to nine months prior to the date you plan to start the business. This will give you time to find a suitable match and give them time to take care of all pre-startup functions, such as establishing your business form and helping you with your business plan.

What to Expect from Professional Services

Legal

You need an attorney with broad-based expertise in business who can help you with such matters as raising capital, legal and tax ramifications and the benefits of various business forms including sole proprietorship, partnership or corporation. Also important are name clearance (to ensure that you are not using a name already designated by another company), legal tips on operating in your desired location, and the ability to file all necessary legal papers and documents needed for financing and establishing your business.

He or she will review contracts and lease agreements and can provide support with collection problems. The lawyer you select should also be willing and able to represent you in the event of any claims that are brought against you or lawsuits you initiate.

Fees

Depending on your lawyer's expertise, reputation and where he/she is located (metropolitan area versus small town, for example), fees will differ dramatically. In a smaller community, lawyers often charge a set rate for the job being done while "city" lawyers typically charge by the hour with fees ranging anywhere from $65 to $250 per hour.

This does not include the extraneous expenses involved, such as the $300 to $1,000 cost of incorporating, depending on the state you operate in. Fees also do not include supplemental costs, such as travel and telephone, incurred by the attorney in the handling of your case.

A good way to get an idea of what to expect in the way of fees in your area is to check with your local chamber of commerce or the state bar association, generally located in the capital city. The bar association may also be able to provide you with information about a particular attorney's reputation and expertise.

When talking with potential attorneys—and when you have found one who is compatible to your needs—always be sure to ask for an outline of expenses and also find out if they are willing to notify you when the fees for a particular job will be exceeded.

Accounting

The accountant you select should, early on, be able to work with you on putting together your business plan, including your projected profit and loss statements, for financing.

Down the line as your business is being established, the accountant will help you set up your books and, once in operation, should handle your tax returns, prepare financial statements and offer financial advice regarding tax matters, cash flow, investments to maximize the use of profits and the tax regulations regarding employees, when you are ready to hire.

Fees

As with attorneys, there is a professional association in your state capital that certifies and maintains records on the reputation and fee structures of accountants. The basis for fee structuring does vary slightly, however, with accountants. Some charge by the hour, others by the day and still others work on a set monthly retainer, based on the estimated amount of time they will be required to spend on your work. Hourly fees average between $25 and $100 depending on expertise and location.

Insurance

Before setting out on your search for an insurance agent, it is advisable to have already established your business form and learned exactly what insurance the law in your area requires you to carry (fire, liability, etc.) And if you will be hiring employees, find out what kind of program you want to offer, as well as what you will need for your own medical and life insurance.

The insurance agent you choose should be familiar with the needs of businesses and business owners, not just the standard life and disability policies. Your insurance needs will change as your business grows and expands (i.e., employee health, workman's compensation, etc.). At that point, you may want to consider key person coverage to insure that a small company can survive if a major partner or employee dies.

There are also a number of pension programs and stock-option programs available in the event you want to offer employees the incentive to increase their participation in the company in exchange for partial "ownership" down the line.

Fees

The fees for your agent's expertise are paid from your premiums, and there should definitely not be any extra charge to you for advice or administration of your insurance policies and programs.

10

TAXES, LICENSES AND PERMITS

As a business owner, you are responsible for the timely report filing and payment of federal, state and local taxes. Whether you have an accountant prepare your returns, or do it yourself, the task will be made much easier if you establish a systematic record-keeping system to keep your records accurate and up-to-date.

This includes maintaining all written documents pertaining to the financial aspect of your business: invoices, bank statements, receipts of any and all business expenses and deposit slips.

One of the easiest ways to keep control of the "paper dragon" is to set up a 9 x 12 inch manila envelope or a file folder for each of the following categories: Paid Bills—both personal and business; sales receipts of every product you've sold or service job performed; inventory records based on ongoing inventory control and quarterly audits; copies of invoices or billing statements that are paid with a separate file for those still due you; receipts for miscellaneous cash purchases; auto and entertainment receipts from travel and promotional activities.

All of these documents must be kept for at least five years to substantiate deductions claimed on your income tax returns in the event of an I.R.S. audit. Make up new file folders or envelopes at the beginning of each year and store the old ones in a safe place.

It is not only a time-consuming task that can take you away from the important job of running your business, but preparing income tax returns, especially for the federal government, has become almost an art form. Tax law is a constantly changing, complicated fact of life. It is strongly recommended that you have an accountant lined up to prepare your taxes and keep you informed of any pertinent changes during the year.

Business Deductions

The deductions that you will most likely qualify for as a business owner include expenses incurred for the operating of business, such as telephone, postage, advertising, bank service charges, travel and expense of conventions, interest, dues to professional organizations and subscriptions to magazines pertaining to your business, among others.

If you have established your business at home, you will be able to deduct that portion of the house used exclusively for business, as well as a percentage of your costs for telephone service and utilities.

Again, because of the complexity and obscurity of many of the deductions, it is best to have a professional do your taxes to ensure you get the full benefits you are entitled to.

The list on the following page provides an overview of the tax returns that may be applicable to your business situation. It is meant only to inform you. Filing requirements will be determined by the type of business, the legal structure (sole proprietorship, partnership or corporation), income from the business, your location, state and local laws and whether or not you have employees.

For example, as the sole proprietor of your business you would probably only be required to file personal federal and state returns based on profit or loss with the appropriate schedules for business expenses, pay sales, self-employment and estimated taxes, local business license fees and sales tax.

Federal Tax Returns

Form 1040: Income tax for Sole Proprietors,Partners or S Corporation shareholders.
Schedule C: Profit (or Loss) from Business or Profession.
Form 1065: Partnership income tax return.
Schedule K-1: Partner's share of Income, Credits, Deductions, etc.
Form 1120: Corporation tax return with applicable support schedules.
Form 2553: S Corporation Filing
Form 1120-S: S Corporation Tax Return
Form 1040ES: Quarterly Estimated Tax for Sole Owner or Partner.
Form 1120W: Quarterly Estimated Tax for Corporation.
Form 940: Federal Unemployment (Social Security) Tax for Sole Owner, Partner, Corporations.
Schedule SE: Annual return of self-employment tax for Sole Proprietor or Partner.

State Income Tax

Each state has corresponding filing requirements; however, form and schedule numbers vary. Contact your State Franchise Tax Board or your accountant for details.

Local Taxes

Taxes will vary from city to city and county to county; however, you may be required to pay city income tax, local sales tax as well as real or personal property taxes. Check with your local government offices for specifics.

Licenses and Permits

To operate your business, you will need permits and licenses based on the requirements in your area and the type of business you are running. You will probably, however, be required to obtain the following documents no matter where you live.

Local Business License

Basically this is simply a fee paid to the city or county in which you are located that allows you to operate your business in that area. Some cities will also require you to pay a percentage of your gross sales every year.

Fictitious Name Statement

This is a registration for protection of your business name. Filing for the fictitious name statement will also involve a city or county-wide search to make sure you are not duplicating an existing name. See details in "Naming Your Business" in this section.

Seller's Permit or Resale Certificate

Required only if you are going to be charging sales tax. Services are often exempt.

Health Permit

Required if you are preparing or distributing food in any manner. Involves an initial inspection and sporadic follow-up inspections by health department officials.

Taxpayer Identification Number

Available from the I.R.S. by filing Form SS-4, in the case of partnerships, S corporations or corporations. Sole proprietors are required to have a taxpayer identification number if they pay wages to one or more employee or file pension or excise tax forms.

Your local governmental offices or your attorney will be able to give you information on the specific licenses and permits, and required fees for each as required in your case.

Legal Structure

As a self-employed business owner, you are required to decide on a legal form of business for tax reporting purposes. There are four basic classifications, as outlined below. If, after reviewing them, you are still unsure of which way to go, it would be advisable to talk with a lawyer about the advantages and disadvantages of each structure for your particular business.

Sole Proprietorships

This is the easiest to establish and the preferred structure for many small business owners. A proprietorship is relatively free from government regulation, as the business has no existence apart from the owner. Profits from the operation of business are treated as personal income for purposes of taxation and your proprietary interest ends when you die or dissolve the business.

The major drawback of a proprietorship is that you are personally liable for any and all claims against the business and undertake the risks of the business to the extent of all assets, whether they are used in the business or personally owned. As a sole proprietor, you will be required to file self-employment tax returns and ordinarily would have to make estimated tax payments on a quarterly basis.

General Partnership

This is also easy to set up and administer. Since responsibilities and capitalization are usually shared by two or more partners, taxation is based on each partner's share of business income and determined by their individual tax rates. Again, claims against the business can be filed against personal assets and financial liability is shared equally by all partners.

Limited Partnership

This structure can be established when one or more people are willing to invest cash or tangible property in the business with active participation in the daily operations. However, there must be at least one general partner who carries unlimited financial liability and usually maintains a full-time managerial position within the company.

The limited partner(s) are liable only for business debts up to the amount of their investment. Although a partnership is not a taxable entity, it must figure its profit or loss and file an annual tax return, which also becomes part of the partners' personal returns.

Corporation

In this structure, stock or shares in the business are sold to investors or stockholders, who then control the company.

The advantage is that corporate stockholders are removed from any liability against personal assets. The most anyone can lose in the event of bankruptcy or a liable claim is their stock.

The privilege of reduced liability, however, creates paperwork (articles of incorporation and annual reports for the state tax commission and federal regulators); expenses (filing and licensing fees) and double taxation (the corporation is taxed on profits, while stockholders and elected officers are taxed individually on wages and/or dividend income).

Subchapter S Corporations

This structure has proved to be a real boon for small business owners who want the benefit of corporate protection from personal liability without double taxation. In a Subchapter S corporation, a maximum of 35 stockholders report their share of corporate income on individual tax returns.

The corporation itself is generally exempt from federal income tax; however, it may be required to pay a tax on excess net passive investment income, capital gains or built-in gains. To structure your company as a Subchapter S corporation, all of the shareholders must consent to the choice.

All businesses, regardless of size, are required to maintain detailed records and file the necessary tax returns. In a corporation, regular meetings must be held. The stockholders elect a board of directors, who establish and monitor corporate policy. The board selects corporate officers to conduct the operations of the business.

Sole proprietorships are the most convenient and least complicated form of business organizations for new business owners, especially in the early stages. As your business grows, you will want to explore the options as a way of protecting your personal assets and increasing the potential for expansion capital.

11

NAMING YOUR BUSINESS

As a pet owner, it is unlikely that you would give your German Shepherd a name like Fifi. It wouldn't suit the dog's image, nor would it be appropriate. The same principle applies to choosing a name for your business.

The name you select for your business can be a tremendous asset when it defines the kind of image you want to project. You want the name to attract and appeal to potential customers, to be easily remembered over that of the competition's, and be appropriate to the type of business you are starting.

Today's consumers are constantly bombarded with advertising as they go about their daily routines. Getting their attention, and holding it long enough for them to make an association between your business name and what you are offering, is imperative.

A memorable moniker can mean the difference between continued growth or a mediocre response from an audience victimized by information overload. (It is, of course, important to remember that your ultimate success depends on well designed advertising, careful planning, and quality products and/or service).

Naming Your Mail Order Lingerie Business

Take some time to think about this, because your company name needs to fulfill several functions beyond identifying you. The name you choose can affect a customer's perceptions of your legitimacy.

It may serve you best to just use your own name, e.g., Mary's Mail Order Lingerie.

Depending on where you live, there may be a number of other mail order lingerie businesses with names that are similar to the one you want. Set yourself apart from the flock. Choose a name that is catchy and descriptive, and then come up with a logo that says something about who you are.

Brainstorming

Start by making a list of all the positive aspects of your business that you can think of, and call on friends and relatives to provide as many as they can come up with. Write down all the possibilities, no matter how funny or unusual they seem. A handy tool for business naming is the thesaurus, which will give you a vast number of options for commonplace names. Consider everything that springs forth from your imagination.

When you have created a list of likely candidates, get together with a group of supportive friends and family members and have a brainstorming session to either pick one of the choices you have come up with or to develop something from the ideas listed. Chances are that within a few hours, you will have a name for your business.

Catchy names are fun to design. However, make sure it isn't so offbeat, cute, or trendy as to risk slipping into obscurity as time passes.

The Fictitious Name Statement

You are required to file a fictitious name statement with the county clerk's office where you will be basing the business. While there, you should be able to do a countywide name check on the spot to see if there are any other businesses in the region using the name you have selected. The filing fee depends on where you live, and must be done within thirty days after you officially open your business.

It will also be necessary to publish the fictitious name in a local newspaper; the cost depends on the circulation of the paper. The county clerk's office will advise you about specific requirements in your area.

If you are starting a business that will be operating in a broader market, statewide or nationally, it is important to have your attorney do a name clearance investigation, which can take from three days to three weeks.

Your Visual Image

After you have selected a name that reflects your business image, the next step is translating it into a visual symbol or logo (logo type) to serve as a signature piece for your business. Often this involves creating a visual interpretation of your company name, but in other cases a graphic symbol or trademark is designed to serve as identification.

Some established corporate trademarks are so familiar that you can immediately identify the company even without seeing or hearing its name.

A good example of this includes the logo of the dog

with his head cocked to one side. The accompanying copy reads "His Master's Voice," and it's a good bet that you recognize this as the logo for RCA. Another effective logo is the avant-garde apple that identifies Apple computer products.

If you do not have the graphic skills necessary to design a logo with impact, get in touch with your nearest art association (listed in the phone book or available through local art supply shops or galleries) or call a near-by college or university. Ask the head of the art department if your design can be given as a class assignment or if he or she could recommend a student to do the job for a small fee. It will give students practical application, and the design can be used later in their portfolios. You can offer cash or a prize for the best design. The students will undoubtedly meet the challenge with enthusiasm and give you a number of good samples and ideas from which to choose.

Selecting a Typeface

Save sample logos and advertisements that use a typeface you like. Type is an extremely important element of logo design and can also pinpoint the precise image you hope to express. Type not only presents the basic message, it can play a powerful role in the overall appearance of your logo and can actually create atmosphere. A chart of some of the more popular typefaces is included at the end of this chapter.

When deciding on a typeface for your logo, visit print shops or typesetting studios and look at their typeface books. They offer both the usual, functional varieties as well as a selection of unique typefaces that can really dress up your logo and subtly portray a specific personality such as dignified, fun, powerful, classic or cutting edge.

Have the logo and your business information (address, phone number, etc.) set in more than the one typeface so that you can see how they will look when printed. Also ask to have them set in both small (10- to 12-point for business cards) and larger (20- to 40-point for letterhead) versions. Once typeset, you will be able to make a final decision about which typeface suits the image you want to project.

Typesetters generally have a minimum fee based on the amount of time they spend on a job, which can vary from $15 per hour in a small city to $50 per hour in a business area, as high as $100 per hour in major metropolitan areas. That's why it's important to shop around.

Word processing specialists or independent desktop publishers can also provide a variety of typefaces and formats at less expense. Since you will only be having a few words typeset, the time and cost required to set them in several different styles should certainly be affordable.

> *Historically, in developing business names, simplicity has scored the highest points. The name you choose should be short, to the point and easy for consumers to pronounce.*

Business Cards and Stationery

The typeface and logo you eventually choose will be used on your letterhead; in your display and telephone advertising; on all promotional materials, including flyers, brochures, and announcements; on your sign; and on statements and invoices.

They will also be used on your business cards, one of the most inexpensive and convenient ways to inform people about your service or product. Once you have had cards printed, be generous. Give one to everyone you meet and always be sure to carry a supply wherever you go.

Most fast-print copy centers are prepared to help you if you decide not to design your own business cards and stationery. They have samples of business forms, letterheads, and cards with various styles to choose from. Make sure that your company name, logo, address, and phone number are included where necessary. If you have a fax and/or toll-free number, be sure those numbers are included. When someone looks at your card or letterhead, it must tell them instantly who you are, what your business is, and how you can be reached.

Sample Typefaces

Arial ABCDEFGHIJ abcdefghij	Futura ABCDEFGHIJ abcdefghij	Helvetica Condensed ABCDEFGHIJ abcdefghij
Benguiat Frisky ABCDEFGHIJ abcdefghij	Futura Light ABCDEFGHIJ abcdefghij	Monaco ABCDEFGHIJ abcdefghij
Bookman ABCDEFGHIJ abcdefghij	**Futura Heavy** **ABCDEFGHIJ** **abcdefghij**	Palatino ABCDEFGHIJ abcdefghij
Bookman Bold **ABCDEFGHIJ** **abcdefghij**	**Futura Extra Bold** **ABCDEFGHIJ** **abcdefghij**	*Palatino Italic* *ABCDEFGHIJ* *abcdefghij*
Brush Script *ABCDEFGHIJ* *abcdefghij*	Garamond ABCDEFGHIJ abcdefghij	**Palatino Bold** **ABCDEFGHIJ** **abcdefghij**
Chicago **ABCDEFGHIJ** **abcdefghij**	**Garamond Bold** **ABCDEFGHIJ** **abcdefghij**	*Park Avenue* *ABCDEFGHIJ* *abcdefghij*
Eras Book ABCDEFGHIJ abcdefghij	*Garamond Bold Italic* *ABCDEFGHIJ* *abcdefghij*	Stone Serif ABCDEFGHIJ abcdefghij
Eras Bold **ABCDEFGHIJ** **abcdefghij**	Geneva ABCDEFGHIJ abcdefghij	*Stone Serif Italic* *ABCDEFGHIJ* *abcdefghij*
Fenice ABCDEFGHIJ abcdefghij	Helvetica ABCDEFGHIJ abcdefghij	Times Roman ABCDEFGHIJ abcdefghij
Fenice Bold **ABCDEFGHIJ** **abcdefghij**	**Helvetica Black** **ABCDEFGHIJ** **abcdefghij**	*Times Italic* *ABCDEFGHIJ* *abcdefghij*

Notes

Key Points:

_____

_____

_____

_____

Personal Thoughts:

_____

_____

_____

_____

_____

_____

_____

_____

Additional Research:

_____

_____

_____

_____

12

PREPARING THE BUSINESS PLAN

Developing your business plan is the most important process you will undertake in your career as an entrepreneur, regardless of the size or type of business you have decided to start.

A well thought-out business plan will serve as a blueprint while your idea turns into a recognizable entity and as it grows into a stable and profitable venture. Too often we hear former small business owners say they probably could have made a success of their business if they had only known what to expect from the beginning . . . and that is where the business plan comes in.

Too many new entrepreneurs are unfamiliar with the importance of planning or consider themselves an exception and feel they can succeed by winging it or dealing with problems as they arise. Not so!

Every business, whether a large commercial or a small home-based venture, needs to analyze its potential, examine strengths and weaknesses and determine the future of the company. It works for the major corporations and it will work for you, especially once you become involved in the day-to-day operations of the business! Having a business plan will give you the freedom to follow the steps you have carefully laid out with regard to budgeting, the success ratio of a product or service, the hiring of employees and other growth decisions.

Advantages of a Business Plan

Once you have made the all-important decision to leave the 9-to-5 world behind, take the plunge and become a business owner, you must devise a specific statement that clearly outlines what you plan to do, when you plan to do it and how you will accomplish the short and long-term goals.

Not only will this keep you on track, it will serve as an indicator of your sincerity and knowledge to others when you go out to find start-up or expansion capital and as the foundation of your financing proposal.

The other advantage is that the actual task of putting your business plan together will help you define and clarify every step of your concept and, if done in a conscientious and objective manner, will point out potential trouble spots that can be addressed before they become a major problem.

If all the necessary components are covered, it will put your business on the road to profit. It is a sure bet that, down the road, if you find your business is not generating the income you had originally projected, it will very likely be because you didn't include one or more of the basic business plan requirements.

Case History

Barbara Ruiz didn't plan on becoming a successful mail order lingerie "tycoon" when she started selling artwork through the mail.

Barbara, a college art teacher, had the idea of selling her students' artwork in a small regional catalog.

Some of her students were supplying needlepoint and fine lace-work done on basic chemises and camisoles. These particular items were selling faster than anything else in her catalog.

"The lingerie items kept selling before I could even mail the catalogs."

Not being one to let an opportunity pass, Barbara started a second catalog containing only lingerie. By buying pieces wholesale and hiring students to add small needlepoint flourishes, she was able to keep her prices at a premium.

"I still enjoy producing the art catalog, but the lingerie book is where I'm making some substantial money!"

Not a Guessing Game

Like any other major project, preparing a business plan involves time and research. It shouldn't be a guessing game. It will be necessary to ask yourself some very specific questions and to answer them thoughtfully and honestly. The business plan is your foundation, so build it carefully to ensure that it works at optimum efficiency for your needs. And make sure it is typed so you, and others, recognize its importance in the professional scheme of your expanding operation.

An important aspect to remember is that your business plan is not cast in stone. In fact, one of the wonderful things about a business plan is that it invites change and revisions as your business changes. This makes it a companion in your success and, by reviewing it regularly, a partner in your progress.

The best way to approach your business plan is to take paper and pen and devote a few hours to coming up with some hard answers. Putting them down on paper will give you all the information you need to write the plan. Of course, you will want to condense your answers to fit into specific segments within the plan, including (in order of appearance) Concept and Feasibility, Legal Structure, Product or Service, Customer Base, Marketing and Production Goals, Personnel (your resume and Entrepreneurial Profile and those of any other key personnel), and Financial Statements.

It is advisable to start each segment on a separate page and to create a table of contents to place in the front. Be sure it is neatly typed, well-written and organized, and bound in a report folder to preserve it and give it a professional quality, especially when using it as a "sales" tool to convince lenders.

Key Questions to Ask Yourself

The first question you must ask yourself is: Why am I interested in this particular business? Probably to be your own boss and make money... independence and income.

This answer is fine as a personal goal, but it isn't going to be good enough if you are planning to approach potential lenders for funding. They will want to see an overview of your business concept, why you are convinced it will be successful and where it fits in the scheme of similar businesses in your town or city.

> *Show me a person with an obsession about succeeding and a solid business plan and I'll show you a good risk.*
>
> *Anonymous*
> *Loan Officer*

The next question you must address is: What is my product or service? This may seem like a ridiculous question since you know your product is mail order lingerie or your service is catering, local sightseeing tours or whatever, but it goes deeper.

Your written response will include details about the service or a description of your product, preferably positive, and with a focus on why customers will be inclined to purchase from you.

Additional questions to analyze should include:

- Why do I believe there is a need for my product or service?
- How do I plan to develop my business over the next five years?
- How much will I charge to ensure value to the customer and profit for myself?
- Who are my suppliers?
- Who are my customers?
- What equipment do I need to start the business?
- How much inventory and supplies do I need for start-up?
- What will it cost?
- Who is my competition and where are they located?
- What are they offering and how can I improve my offer to attract customers?
- What changes are occurring in my marketing area that will impact my business in the future?
- What are my estimated sales figures for each of the next five years? (A "guesstimate" based on researching similar businesses in the area)
- How will I advertise and promote my business (including estimated costs of doing so)?
- How and where is my product going to be manufactured?
- What is involved in the production—materials, labor, costs?
- Where will my service be performed?
- What equipment is required for my service (costs for leasing versus purchasing)?
- What are other overhead expenses (rent, employees, etc.)?
- How many people will be involved in the business and what are their qualifications?

• If I don't have employees, am I qualified to run the business myself? Will I need outside assistance?

By talking with people in similar businesses, suppliers and direct competitors, as well as your local chamber of commerce, you will gather a great deal of information, both positive and negative, about your potential business. People love to talk about their success and, if you ask the right questions, their failure, as well.

Become an investigative reporter for a few days while preparing to write your business plan and it's guaranteed that you will obtain plenty of good, solid information. A SCORE representative through the Small Business Administration can also offer assistance, or give you resources that will help you develop a realistic business plan.

Trade associations, listed in reference books available at your local library, can provide you with invaluable details on industry facts and figures, such as the percentage of gross sales that should be spent on advertising, the percentage that is typically paid for rent in your particular business and how to price your product or service.

The final item to include in this section of your business plan, when and if presenting it for financing, is a personal résumé, designed to emphasize your business management experience, in general, and your expertise within the area of your chosen business, specifically.

Describe the job duties for every job you have held, including any special aspects that pertain directly to the business. If you cannot prepare the résumé, it is worth the $25 to $40 to have it done professionally.

Financial Statements

Once you have written your overview and description sheets, it is time to get down to numbers. This is the key to your business plan and, unfortunately, the area where many entrepreneurs get bogged down. But without an understanding about the numbers involved, you can never expect to be a good manager and really shouldn't be surprised if you run into money problems within the first year.

Again, utilizing the resources indicated earlier—chamber of commerce, trade associations, etc.—you will need to work up your financial pages to include the following components, which most lenders will want to see spread out for between one and five years.

Projected operating expenses: Materials, advertising, salaries for employees or outside labor, and other expenses directly related to the cost of doing business.

Estimate of gross (before tax) sales revenue: Based on research figures from trade associations and what the local market dictates, if the business is not yet operating or, if open, how many items or hours of service you plan to sell and the average price.

How you arrived at the figures for these statements: Generally you would base your figures on assumptions made about the number of months of operation, estimated number of sales and the average amount versus the cost of each sale.

Cost of equipment and furnishings: Get estimated quotes, whether planning to purchase or lease these items.

Cost of materials for production: if applicable, or maintenance on equipment needed to run the business.

Additional operating expenses: Rent, telephone and other utilities, business taxes and license fees, office supplies, even decorating costs and a category called "other" to provide a cushion for unexpected expenses.

Balance sheet: Shows assets, such as equipment and operating capital you already have, and liabilities or debts and expenses (if the business has not yet started, this would be a personal balance sheet indicating your net worth; listing all possessions of any value plus cash, stock and other holdings minus all financial responsibilities).

Leasehold improvements: If you are planning to rent a commercial location or redesign a room within your home strictly for business, estimate cleaning and restoration costs in this statement.

By investing the time and energy into this portion of the business plan, you will absorb the numbers into your consciousness and be able to recognize, at a glance, when your costs exceed your profit margin or when you are in a position to start making expansion moves.

If money matters are absolutely beyond your comprehension at this point, it would pay to hire someone to work along with you in developing the financial pages of the plan. There are business consultants and accountants who will probably charge you a substantial amount, or you can approach the accounting or business department of the nearest college and see if there is a qualified student available to help you.

No matter whom you find to assist you, be sure to stay involved in the process... the discipline and hard work will guarantee success.

13

THE MATTER OF MONEY: FINANCING ALTERNATIVES

Starting your business without having sufficient capital is setting yourself up for problems from the very beginning. Undercapitalization is cited as one of the major reasons why businesses do not succeed, and this is the result of bad planning.

If you research and record all the goals, marketing data, equipment and supply requirements and financial needs of your venture before actually opening the doors, you will be able to see at a glance how much you need to get going and why you need it. That way, there will be no surprises and no reason that your business should suffer from lack of capitalization.

It is important to have the financial resources to cover all your preliminary planning and start-up costs, including expenses incurred to research the feasibility of your business and those required to set up shop, from equipment and supplies to advertising and utility set-up charges. You will also need a surplus to carry you over personally until the business becomes productive.   The Cash Flow Statement and Projected Expense Charts provided in chapter 7 will help you determine these expenses.

If, after drawing up your business plan (which is covered in chapter 12), you find that your personal resources are not enough to open the business, there are other options available.   The four most common methods include: (a) starting the business on a part-time basis while holding a full-time job to cover expenses, (b) taking on a limited partner, (c) going to friends or family members for the money you need or (d) applying for a loan through a commercial lender or the Small Business Administration (SBA).

There are, of course, pros and cons to each of these options.

Starting Out Part Time

Starting your business on a part time or "moonlighting" basis is a decision that must be made based on the nature of the business. If you are planning to capitalize on your skills in upholstering, for example, you should have no trouble building up the business at night and on weekends.

It is perfectly feasible to start small, using your garage or home as your production facility and purchasing an answering machine for potential customers to leave a message while you are at your regular job. When you get home, you simply call them back to discuss prices and arrange a time when it is convenient to pick up the piece of furniture to be upholstered.

On the other hand, if you are planning to start a temporary help agency, for example, it would be in your best interest to go into it on a full-time, dedicated basis, as your potential customers are going to want fast results. They will call someone else if they are even slightly discouraged, such as getting a recorded message when they call.

Starting part time will be practical in some businesses, but before exploring it as an option you must figure out if your limited availability will affect your credibility, if you really have the time and energy to work at a regular job and try to build a business (not to mention family responsibilities) and whether your ultimate goal is to be self-employed or just to earn a few extra dollars to supplement your base income.

Considering a Partner

Going into business with a limited partner who will put up the money you need while stepping into the background to let you run the business the way you see fit is a feasible idea. You must be sure, however, to have your lawyer draw up a precise partnership agreement that covers every eventuality. Partnerships are typically entered into with the best intentions and the unwavering belief that the business will be successful.

Since this is not always the case—and even if it were—it is a businesslike move to ensure that such aspects as decision making, distribution of profits and losses, contributions of partners and handling disputes and changes are outlined and approved by all the partners.

Friends and Family

The third option, raising capital through friends or family members, is probably one of the most often exercised methods. The advantage of getting a loan from a personal contact is that they know you, undoubtedly trust your ability to make the business go and won't require much in the way of substantiating paperwork, such as complex loan applications, financial statements, etc. In addition, you will most likely be able to negotiate a small interest rate on the loan.

The major disadvantage, according to entrepreneurs who have taken this route, is if the friendly lender decides he or she want to provide input on the care and maintenance of your business. This problem, however, can be eliminated by a "cards-on-the-table" discussion prior to accepting the loan. In other words, choose your investor carefully!

The second problem has to do with repayment of the loan. Even though you have a loose agreement in writing with your lender, because of friendship or family ties there may come a point when Uncle Bill needs that $10,000 tomorrow to take care of a personal obligation. You can't possibly come up with the money overnight, Uncle Bill gets angry and much of the family turns against you.

> *Money brings some happiness.*
>
> *But, after a certain point, it just brings more money.*
>
> *Neil Simon*

The flip side of the coin is if the business fails and you are unable to pay Uncle Bill or your old college pal the $5,000 he or she put up. These are unpleasant situations, so you must be sure in the beginning to think about the importance of the relationship you have with the potential lender, how the best and the worst of situations would affect the situation and whether you then could justify asking for money.

Commercial Lenders

If you are not able to, or decide against approaching friends or relatives for financial assistance, the next step is a bank, a savings & loan or a credit union. Before approaching any of these commercial lenders you must have carefully developed your business plan, which will include the following documents.

a) A resume or statement outlining your background and capability to operate the business, plus a similar statement about any key employees or partners in the business;

b) A statement of business and personal goals;

c) A description about the business, including research about the market for your product or service;

d) Details on how the business is going to be structured (sole proprietorship, partnership, corporation, non-profit status);

e) A projection of profit and loss for a minimum of one year, which forces you to do your homework and investigate how similar businesses in similar locations are doing, and

f) An outline of how much money you need—and why—to keep the business solvent and to support yourself and your family for at least a year.

In addition, you will be required to provide a personal balance sheet that lists your assets, such as property, a car, etc., and liabilities like your mortgage payments, credit card debts, etc., and a credit application thath outlines your personal financial history (so they can make a determination on your ability to pay back the loan). The lender will follow through by requesting a credit report from an independent agency, such as TRW, to help them make their decision.

The main thing to remember when applying for a loan

with a commercial institution is that lenders aren't as concerned about how much money they loan as they are about how and when they are going to get the money back!

Approaching a Lender

Once you have your business plan and other paperwork prepared, decide which lending institution you want to approach. Certainly, if you have a stable record with a checking or savings account at your regular bank or S&L, that is the place to try first. Set up an appointment with the bank manager or loan officer to make your request and explain why you feel your business venture is worth their investment.

Be aware, however, that banks are more likely to provide you with a loan payable within five or ten years, as opposed to savings & loans, which are more interested in long-term loans, such as for mortgages. Credit unions operate in a similar manner to banks; however, you generally have to be a member. If you do belong to a credit union, it could be your best bet as they offer lower interest rates and can be more flexible in their determinations.

If, for some reason, you do not want to run a loan through your bank, consider talking with other local small business owners. Very often, they can steer you to a regional, often independently owned bank or S&L that is empathetic to and supportive of new businesses. In that case, proceed as mentioned above and arrange a meeting with the manager or loan officer.

Present your case in a friendly, yet professional manner. Be realistic and honest about your needs. Do not underbid because of fear that you will not get a loan if you ask for too much. It is always better to start with a higher figure than you actually need so you have a strong negotiating edge.

In addition, most lenders have a pretty good idea about start-up and operating costs of new businesses and are much less likely to give you, and risk losing, a small loan for a business they know calls for more capital. They will be more willing to work with you if you are realistic and obviously knowledgeable about your needs.

If, after your first try, the answer is no, ask for reasons why you are being turned down so you can restructure your presentation. Turn opposition into a learning tool to re-define and polish your material and to develop new negotiating strategies.

There are always other potential lenders you can approach, and the law of averages dictates that you will get your loan if the idea is solid and it is apparent that you have researched the feasibility of starting a business in your particular area.

The SBA

The Small Business Administration (SBA) often goes where no other lender will tread and, as such, is a lender of last resort.

The SBA is a government agency that is well known for providing financing to entrepreneurs who have been repeatedly turned down by commercial lenders (which in fact must be the case before the SBA will consider backing you).

After your loan request with a commercial institution has been denied, you can file an application with the nearest branch of the SBA. It is a good idea to make an appointment with a SCORE (Service Corps of Retired Executives) representative, who volunteers his or her time to the SBA-SCORE program to advise new and established business owners. Your SCORE representative will be able to lead you through the complex paperwork required by the SBA before they make a decision.

In addition, the SCORE volunteers are usually straightforward, knowledgeable men and women who will walk through your business plans with you and offer constructive suggestions. Once the paperwork is completed, a commercial lender will make the loan under the SBA Lender Certification Program, knowing that the government is willing to insure it.

This option is recommended only after you have been turned down by three or more banks, because of the time factor involved in gaining approval and also because of the extensive follow-up reports required of SBA. It is, however, a viable option and one that has helped thousands of dedicated entrepreneurs realize their goals.

Venture Capitalists

Money is available to businesses that are already established and seeking working or expansion capital from groups of investors known as venture capitalists. These groups can vary from a few local businessmen with money to invest to major investment companies connected with large corporations or financial organizations.

Venture capital is not like a straightforward business loan. It is usually dependent on a minimum $100,000 investment and, therefore, is not suited to every business situation. Typically, venture capitalists are interested in companies that have a track record, a proven position in the market and a solid growth projection.

But, like a bank or other lending association, venture capitalists want to see a written business plan and a prospectus of future projections. They are looking at your background, the market, the kind of funding you want and your past financial record. Since venture capitalists are looking to earn from 10 to 15% on their investment over a relatively short period, they will want to spend a great deal of time talking with you and your associates, customers and suppliers.

Before considering venture capital, we advise discussing it carefully with an attorney who can help you investigate different groups and figure out the best investment structure for you and the organization you choose, and work with their attorney on drawing up an agreement that protects you, since many venture capitalists will want to become a part owner in your company.

This is an option to be considered only when your company is well-established and undergoing rapid growth pains and should be approached with great understanding of the situation.

Other Financing Options

Loan companies are an additional source of funding. However, interest rates are high and they will generally want to have substantial collateral, such as the equity in your house, on record before making a loan.

Insurance companies. Your insurance carrier may be willing to make an investment in your small business, using your insurance policy as collateral. Or, you may even have enough cash value in your policy, depending on the face amount, to provide you with substantial start-up capital. If this is the case, you will be required only to pay quarterly or semi-annual interest payments on the cash value you have taken out.

Factoring. In this instance, a factoring company "buys" your accounts receivables and advances you a percentage of the full amount due. This is a viable option for well-established service companies that work on a billing basis.

Co-signer. If you have a relative or friend who is already an established business owner or, at least, a homeowner with a solid credit rating, it might be worth your while to ask if he or she would co-sign on a loan application with you. Although you are still responsible for repayment of the loan, the bank is assured that, in the event you default for any reason, the co-signer will guarantee the obligation. It is often difficult to find someone who will do this, but again it doesn't hurt to ask, especially if it is a last resort option.

Starting Small

Even if you know your particular business is valid and that you have the ability to make it succeed, be certain that your business plan is realistic. If you have chosen to start a business on a grand scale but have minimal capital and little business experience, it may be best to begin a smaller, less elaborate operation at first.

You'll require less "seed money" and put yourself in a low-risk position while learning the ropes and seeing if you can handle all the variables of business ownership as it grows.

Smaller businesses have proven to be a great way to learn the successful methods, as well as a vehicle for ironing out the many small details that are often overlooked until you actually start taking care of day-to-day situations. The profits you gain from a smaller venture can be used to expand or invest in bigger business ideas. And, an added bonus is that when you are ready to approach investors or lending institutions, you will be able to show them that you already have a solid track record and a working knowledge of business procedures.

What to Do When Asking for Money

1. **Be sure to ask.** This may seem like a gross statement of the obvious, but you would be amazed at the number of small business owners we talk to who never ask because they are afraid of being turned down.

Unless you are independently wealthy and pursuing

your business as a humanitarian effort, it is unlikely that you are in a position to run your business and earn enough money to support you, your family and the operation—especially during the first year. Remember the old adage: It takes money to make money.

If you run a low-budget business you will probably get low-budget response. If you are determined to make it work, be sure you have sufficient capital to make it work the right way. Fear is often a factor: "I don't want to ask in case they say no." Well, that's the worst thing that can happen. But, if you persevere and are serious about your venture, someone will inevitably say yes!

And don't overlook friends and family; they can be your most ardent cheerleaders and supporters if you have given them reason in the past to believe you are responsible and determined to succeed.

2. Know how much you need. Lenders are familiar with the financial demands of business operation and will respect your request if you have obviously done your homework and can talk sensibly about your needs.

3. Be direct and confident. If you believe in your business and in your ability to make it work, others will be convinced. Never apologize for mistakes you feel you have made in the past and do not present the pathetic picture of someone who could make everything work if they just had enough money.

Simply present the facts, even if they include revealing an error in judgment you have made somewhere along the line, and assure the lender that they will be making a smart decision by investing in you.

4. Think positively. If you need $50,000, ask for $50,000. Never underestimate the potential to provide. Even if you are approaching family members, you may be surprised to find that dear Cousin Fred has a $250,000 nest egg socked away. Anyway, it is easier to negotiate and deal with one lender for a single amount than it is to keep paperwork and relationships strong with several, all of whom have contributed a little to the pot.

5. **Ask again.** If they trusted you once and you have lived up to the stipulations of the contract, ask again and that goes for commercial lending institutions as well as friends and relatives. A proven record is what it's all about and if you have established yours, keep it active.

6. **Know when to borrow.** If you have worked out your business plan and know you can survive while getting the business off the ground, start exploring your financing options ahead of time. Don't wait until the last minute; this will force you to act frantically and could put you in the position of accepting a less than favorable situation. The same theory applies if your business is already established. By examining your financial position on a regular basis, you will be able to project how much you will need at a given point for expansion purposes. Be prepared.

7. **Don't borrow if it is not necessary.** Many businesses can be started for under $500. This is called "starting on a shoestring." Services, for example, often rely strictly on the owner's knowledge and expertise and can be set up quickly and inexpensively.

If this is the case with the business you have in mind, then try to avoid borrowing capital. It can be an expensive and timely proposition. In addition, if, after a projected period of time, the business is showing the kind of profit you can work with while growing, then the smart decision is to utilize the funds and put them back into the operation.

Establishing Credit

Is it possible to get a loan even if you have never established credit? Yes, it is. Many people in this country still prefer to pay cash, rather than incur high interest charges on loans or credit cards. They can still qualify for a loan based on personal assets or by having a friend or relative with a good credit rating who is willing to co-sign. This puts the obligation on the co-signer, so be sure the terms of the loan are clearly spelled out in a written agreement to the satisfaction of everyone involved in the transaction.

However, if your personal assets are minimal and you cannot find a co-signer, the best bet is to put off starting the business for four to six months while you establish credit. The best place to start is with a major department store such as Sears or J.C. Penney's.

They issue credit cards based on a very simple examination of your income and employment history. Charge about $100 worth of merchandise when you receive the card and pay it off according to the schedule provided. Within a few months, you will have proven yourself to be credit worthy, which will greatly improve your chances of getting a loan from a lending institution.

Another way to establish credit—and credibility—is to open a checking account at the bank you have decided to approach for a loan. They generally require a minimum deposit of between $50 and $100. Make it a point to meet the branch manager and/or the loan officer and to establish an ongoing relationship with them by stopping by to say hello when you are in the bank.

Within a few months, apply for a small personal loan, working with your new acquaintance, of course. Make your payments according to the prearranged schedule. Then when you are ready to request a more substantial amount of money to cover your start-up expenses, you will be recognized as a customer with a loan history at that institution.

14

RECORD KEEPING: YOUR BUSINESS LIFELINE

The motivating factor in any business is profit, which can be explained as the money left over after all the bills, for everything from supplies to rent and salaries to taxes, are paid.

Building a profitable business is not something that can be left to chance; it must be planned, and a systematic method of record keeping must be developed to help you control income and expenses.

You should expect that during the early days of your business, your profits are going to be minimal as you become established. But it is possible, with even simple record-keeping procedures, to prepare yourself for lean periods and control day-to-day expenses to ensure that you are, at least, breaking even. In addition, financial records are required for tax purposes and dealing with them systematically can eliminate an incredibly overwhelming task at tax time.

Record Keeping Can Be Simple

Some people cringe at the thought of record keeping or feel it is a waste of valuable time. Usually, these attitudes are based on a lack of knowledge and the feeling that it is an overwhelming task. There is, however, no other way to analyze your cash flow and make sure you are pricing products or services high enough to realize a profit.

In actuality, record keeping is not such a complicated process. If you have ever balanced a checkbook or planned a household budget, you have basically done several of the same steps necessary when implementing a bookkeeping system for your business. And the good news is that keeping your records does not have to be either complicated or time consuming.

We know of entrepreneurs who opt for total simplicity by using the "shoebox" method—every sales record, receipt for expenses and bank statement gets tossed into a box. This system has two distinct drawbacks. One may not become apparent until tax time, when you attempt to wade through the paper to prepare your tax return. (If you hire an accountant to do your taxes, it shouldn't come as a surprise if an additional "combat fee" has been added to the bill.)

The other, more critical drawback is that it is virtually impossible to maintain an accurate picture of your financial situation when you stockpile, rather than record, business transactions. In order to understand your cash flow, it is important to be able to see what monies have come in, what you have paid out, current balances and outstanding debts.

In fact, you should be able to answer the following questions with just a quick review of your records:

- What was my income last year (week or month)?
- What were my expenses?

- How do income and expenses compare with last year (week or month)?
- What was my profit (or loss) last year (week or month)?
- Where can I cut back on expenses?
- Who and how much do I currently owe on outstanding debts?
- Who owes me money and how much?
- What are my assets, liabilities and net worth?
- Is my inventory in line with demand?
- How much cash do I have available?
- How much credit?
- Am I able to pay myself this month (week)?
- Are my figures in line with projected financial goals?

The primary documents that you need to be able to answer most of these questions are a Cash Journal, a Balance Sheet and a Bank Reconciliation. A simple single-entry system, as indicated on the following pages, in which to record disbursements (cash paid out) and receipts (cash taking in) forms the base of your record-keeping.

Double-Entry Bookkeeping

Your accountant will probably utilize a double-entry system, which involves recording each transaction twice: once as a debit (on the left column of the ledger) and once as a credit (the right column of the ledger). For example, if you were to sell a product for $100, the transactions recorded in a double-entry system would be as follows:

The $100 would be written as a credit in your Sales account, since merchandise is going out of the business and $100 would be recorded as a debit in your Cash account since money was coming into the business.

This is a complex and time-consuming process that is often best left to an accountant, as he or she will need the information to create a monthly Trial Balance and other financial statements, including your year-end tax reports.

Single-Entry Bookkeeping

You can, however, have your accountant's office set up a simple single-entry system for you that will tie in directly with their requirements. Or, check out the standardized bookkeeping systems, which provide all the necessary forms and documents in a bound book, stocked by stationery stores.

One of the most widely accepted, ready-made systems is the Dome Simplified Monthly Bookkeeping Record. It contains forms for recording monthly income and expenses, summary sheets from which you can create a balance sheet and listings of legal deductions for income tax reporting. Instructions are included.

In addition, the trade association for your field should be able to provide you with systems developed exclusively for use in the industry, which you can use "as-is" or adapt according to specific circumstances within your business.

The final method is to purchase a Cash Journal book and set up your own monthly system, as outlined below for Office Assistance, a small typing service, which has been operating for one month. Any of the above mentioned methods are acceptable, as long as you understand the entry process and can "read" the results.

Make Record Keeping a Daily Task

The easiest way (short of paying someone else) to be sure your records are kept up-to-date is to incorporate the task into your daily or weekly routine. Many small business owners make it a habit to enter their sales, expenses and other financial information at the end of each working day. It keeps them continually aware of their financial situation and ensures that there will never be any unexpected cash-flow surprises. The process probably takes no more than

15 minutes for normal transactions, but will save hours of pencil-pushing and frustration down the line. And, more important, you'll know where you stand financially.

Setting Up the Books

Using Office Assistance, a secretarial service, as an example, we can examine the various elements required for basic record-keeping duties.

Bill Miller, president of Office Assistance, has been in business for one month. Two months ago, he opened a new business bank account with $10,000.00, his start-up capital from a personal savings account.

At the same time, he rented a small office in a downtown building for $350.00 a month, but had to pay first month rent and a deposit of the last month's rent, for a total outlay of $700.00.

> ## Debit & Credit in Bookkeeping
>
> ### Debits include
> - Cash receipts
> - Purchases
> - Expenses, such as rent and wages
>
> ### Credits include:
> - Cash payments
> - Sales of services or merchandise.
> - Earnings, including interest earned

His fictitious name statement, which he got approved through the local county clerk's office, ran $10.00 and publishing it in a regional newspaper cost $45.00.

The initial month's lease and a deposit on a state-of-the-art typewriter cost him $275.00, plus $50.00 for a maintenance agreement. However, he will own the $2,000 typewriter when his payment schedule is completed.

He found a brand new calculator at a garage sale for $25.00 and is going to use a desk, table, lamp and chairs brought from home (value $350.00) to decorate the office.

Phone installation was $150.00, but he purchased a two-line telephone for $79.50.

An artist friend designed his logo and letterhead on a computer for only $25 and a $6.95 lunch. He had his stationery ($35.00), business cards ($60.00) and brochures ($23.50) produced through a local copy shop for a total of $118.50.

A 2 x 2 inch display ad in the local newspaper cost him $370.00 for a week, and he is planning to mail 100 of his brochures to local businesses selected from the phone book. Stamps cost $25.00 for the mailing. Office supplies, including typing paper, staples, paper clips, etc., set him back $45.00. A journal for record keeping cost $7.95.

He purchased a packet of invoices for $5.95 and, during the first month, has billed and been paid $700.00. However, he has two accounts who still owe him a total of $400. Bill dutifully records information in his cash journal at the end of each working day. He uses source documents, including his checkbook register, receipts from cash purchases and billing invoices as the basis for his entries. The two pages following are for May (prior to opening the doors of his business) and June (his first actual month in business).

Office Assistance
Cash Journal for May

Date	Check # Invoice #	Detail	(Debit) Expense	(Credit) Income
5/1	100	Rawlins Real Estate (Rent & dep)	$700.00	
5/5	101	County Clerk (Fictitious Name)	10.00	
5/7	102	The Herald (publishing FNS)	45.00	
5/9	103	Ed's Keyboards (IBM 1-mo. & dep)	275.00	
5/9	104	Ed's Keyboards (Maint. agreement)	50.00	
5/12	105	Mary Smith (Calculator purchase)	25.00	
5/18	106	Telephone company (line installation)	150.00	
5/20	107	Phone Store (2-line phone)	79.50	
5/22	108	Ray Brown (logo design)	25.00	
5/24	Cash	The Hungry Dog (lunch/Ray Brown)	6.95	
5/28	109	The Copy Spot (brochures, cards, etc.)	35.00	
5/29	110	The Herald (advertising)	370.00	
		Total Income & Expense (May)	$1,771.45	$0.00

Office Assistance
Cash Journal for June

Date	Check # Invoice #	Detail	(Debit) Expense	(Credit) Income
6/4	111	U.S.P.O (Stamps for mailing)	$ 25.00	
6/6	112	Office Stationers (supplies, invoices, etc.)	58.90	
6/7	A1	W. Smith		$ 62.50
6/8	A2	Art Association		112.50
6/9	A3	T. Williams		22.00
6/9	113	Judy Miller (typing fee)	100.00	
6/10	A4	Bank of Cutterville		75.00
6/10	A5	WKTR-FM		120.50
6/13	A6	J. Johnson		43.50
6/15	114	Rawlins Real Estate (rent)	350.00	
6/15	A7	C. Lewis		73.50
6/15	A8	R. Swell		90.00
6/16	115	Judy Miller (typing fee)	100.00	
6/19	A9	W. Smith		52.50
6/23	116	Judy Miller (typing fee)	100.00	
6/26	117	Phone company (bill)	15.90	
6/27	A10	K. Black		48.00
6/30	118	Judy Miller (typing fee)	100.00	

Total Income & Expense (June) $765.90 $700.00

Bill's expenses for May and June were $2,537.35. Of course, part of that is for start-up expenses, such as deposits on his rent and typewriter, installation costs and one-time fictitious name filing and publishing. His income for the first month was $700. By deducting his expenses from his income, he can see that, at the moment, his business is showing a loss of $1,837.35.

Although Bill has been in business for only a month, he is curious about his company's financial worth and decides to work up a balance sheet to get the answer. The calculation, as indicated in the following example, is the amount owned (assets) minus the amount due to creditors (liabilities), which equals his worth.

Balance Sheet as of June 30

Assets		Liabilities	
Cash on hand & in bank	$ 8,162.54	Ed's Keyboards	$ 1,725.00
(Capital balance & June Income)		*(Balance on IBM)*	
Office Equipment	2,104.50	Unpaid rent *(July)*	350.00
(includes full value of IBM		Taxes *(estimated)*	75.00
even though not paid off)			
Office Furniture	350.00		
Accounts Receivable		**Liabilities**	$ 2,150.00
(outstanding invoices			
for work already done)	400.00		
Total Assets	$11,017.04	*CAPITAL	$ 8,867.04
		Total Liabilities	$11,017.04

The figure Bill is most interested in is the *CAPITAL amount in the Liabilities column. This is the amount remaining after what Bill owes is subtracted from his current assets and is what his business is worth at the end of

June. In other words, if he decided to try to sell his business right now, he could realistically ask that amount as a sales price. Of course, Bill probably wouldn't get that amount because he has not yet become established enough to warrant someone buying the business, unless he or she were looking for a "turnkey" operation—in other words, a business he or she could just walk into and get going immediately.

This information is valuable when Bill goes to apply for expansion capital or for credit on future purchases he plans to make, i.e., a photocopier, a computer and new furniture. His balance sheet will change each time he prepares it (probably quarterly in the future) as business increases, bringing in more income and reducing his debts.

In the meantime, the balance sheet gives Bill a tool to use when comparing the financial standing of his business this month against future months and years. It also keeps him current on what he owns, whom he owes money to and his major sources of income.

The same procedure is used in developing a personal balance sheet, which possibly would be needed to establish credibility when applying for a loan. Assets would include furniture, automobiles, jewelry, your home and other tangibles, while liabilities would consist of outstanding loans and other major debts.

Bank Statement Reconciliation

Another important step that Bill must handle monthly is reconciling his bank statement against his checkbook register. He simply marks off the checks in his register that have cleared per the statement and the depositsthat have been credited, and deducts any service charges for the previous month from his balance.

Bill then adds up all the outstanding checks—those listed in his register that have not cleared by the closing date indicated on the bank statement—and deducts them from the balance indicated on his bank statement. He adds up any deposits that have not yet been credited to his account and then adds them to the balance, as indicated below.

Balance per bank statement	$ 7,953.44
Plus: Deposits not credited	+ 325.00
Minus: Outstanding checks	- 115.90
New Balance	$ 8,162.54

The new balance figure should match that listed in his checkbook register and, in this case, it does. If, however, the statement and the register did not reconcile, Bill would have a customer representative at the bank review his statement and banking activity for the past month.

15

PRICING IN GENERAL

One of the toughest problems that small business owners face is establishing prices that, on one hand, the market will bear while, on the other, will cover overhead and guarantee a profit.

Often new business owners give the business away to get sales, but this is not an advisable practice. Realistic pricing indicates your confidence in what you are selling, and if you value your service, so will the customer.

Today's consumer realizes that they can't get something worthwhile for nothing, so don't be afraid to establish prices that will work toward your profit goals.

Pricing Guidelines

Several factors must be taken into consideration when setting prices:

a) **The cost of goods sold.** In the case of a retail or wholesale operation, this is the amount originally paid for the goods, while for a manufacturer, it involves the cost of producing the goods. In the case of a service business, overhead expenses and equipment costs must be taken into account.

b) **The nature of the product or service.** Uniqueness and demand come into play here. In the case of goods with a stable level of demand, such as bread or auto repair, the raising or lowering of prices will have little effect. However, when demand is high for goods that are hard to get, the price can realistically be set anywhere the owner wants.

c) **The competition.** Recognize what your competition is charging, for often this will guide pricing within a certain region. However, if a competitor is charging what you feel is an unrealistic price—either more or less—for a product or service, you owe it to yourself to find out why. Then set your prices according to all of the factors outlined here.

Even if they are higher than the competitor consumers will pay the price if you can offer an advantage, such as a friendly atmosphere, convenient hours or some other benefit not provided by the competition.

d) **Company policy.** This encompasses a number of things, including your location, your position in the marketplace, the additional services offered, and takes it into account your personal philosophy about business and your role in it.

e) **Market strategy.** Should you go for large volume at low prices or for low volume at high prices? That is the bottom line in considering market strategy. As a small business owner, you will likely opt for low volume and higher prices since the alternative involves having the resources, including labor, display room, distribution channels, etc., to move large volumes of product or perform major service tasks.

f) Customers. What will the market bear? In other words, what are your customers willing to pay for your products or services?

People expect prices that are fair; if you are planning to charge overinflated rates you had better be a top-notch salesperson or offer something so unusual that the price won't matter.

Although there are differences between establishing prices for retail operations, wholesale products, manufacturing and services, the basic formula for price setting is:

> **Labor + Materials + Overhead + Profit Margin = Selling Price**

However, before setting prices on goods or services, it is extremely important to understand the concept of the break-even point. Many small business owners operate on an overall profit-loss basis without realizing the importance of cost accounting. Being aware of such factors as your break-even point, markup and profit margin can tell you which areas of your business are profitable and which are causing a drain.

Understanding Break-Even

The break-even point is the minimum amount you must charge in order to cover all expenses incurred for the production and promotion of your goods and/or services without losing or making money. In other words, any income that is above the break-even point is considered to be profit and anything below it is a loss.

To find your break-even point, you must first total all of your operating costs, including materials and labor, equipment lease or purchase payments, advertising, utilities, office supplies and any incidentals such as gasoline, maintenance, postage, etc.

Generally, this is computed for a particular period of time, such as six months or a year. However, if your business is still in the early stages of operation, you can use the estimated figures on your projected expenses statement and "guesstimate" costs for materials and labor.

For example, the monthly expenses for a hypothetical cake decorating business total $300 a month. You want to know what the break-even point would be if you sell an average of 20 cakes per month. The calculation is as follows:

$$\$300 \text{ (expenses)} \div 20 \text{ cakes} = \$15.00$$

In order to break even, that is, without losing money or realizing a profit, you must charge a minimum of $15 for each cake sold.

The same process can be used to analyze the break-even point on a weekly basis. First you determine your annual expenses by multiplying the $300 by 12 months, which would give you $3,600 per year.

The calculation to find the weekly break-even point is:

$$\$3,600 \text{ (expenses)} \div 52 \text{ weeks} = \$69.23$$

Therefore, you must earn $69.23 per week to operate the business without losing money and without realizing a profit.

Stay Informed

Knowing your break-even point is one of the greatest favors you can do for yourself as a business owner. It tells you how much you must charge for your products or services and serves as an invaluable tool in setting prices that will help you realize a profit.

Keep in mind, however, that the break-even point is a variable figure. Since it depends on production and overhead costs, plan to reevaluate periodically to make sure your prices reflect any changes.

Labor Costs

Labor costs, obviously, are the expenses incurred for the actual work done to manufacture or sell a product or to perform a service. Think of them as wages or salaries. Small business owners often end up working for free because they fail to set a wage for themselves. Despite the fact that you want to reinvest all of the income received back into the business for awhile, it is imperative that you establish a fixed salary amount for yourself when figuring operating expenses.

If you have set aside a survival fund to carry you through the first six months or so of operation, you may want to defer your salary until the business becomes solvent; however, you should still figure the amount into your expenses. Otherwise, you may find the prices you set are too low to justify making a profit from the onset.

It is much easier to set realistic prices from the beginning than it is to raise them later in an attempt to make up the difference. Remember, your time and skills are the cornerstone of your business, so think of paying yourself as you would any valuable employee.

Setting Retail Prices

If you are manufacturing items to sell at retail prices, without using a middleman, the following formula is a good basis to start with when establishing a selling price for your inventory of goods.

> 1/3 Labor + 1/3 Materials & Overhead + 1/3 Profit = Selling Price

You need a starting point. One place to start is with your labor costs. If, for example, the monetary value of your time and effort (labor) in producing an item is $6, you allocate $6 for material and overhead and an additional $6 as profit for a total selling price of $18.

If materials and overhead are costing more, you can: (a) boost the price accordingly, (b) review your expenses and find ways to cut back on material costs, such as finding a less expensive supplier or (c) utilize a portion of the profit margin to cover the balance. Of the three options, (b) is the best way to go.

You must also remember that when you are producing mass quantities of an item, your costs will be reduced because of price breaks on supplies and reduced labor costs per unit. You're then able to structure your selling price according to previously mentioned pricing factors, such as competition and demand for the product.

> *Money is a sixth sense which makes it possible for us to enjoy the other five senses.*
>
> *Richard Ney*

If you are starting a retail business that relies on selling products you purchase at wholesale, you may have some of your prices set for you by what the competition is doing or recommendations made by the wholesaler.

However, there will still be items that you must price your-self.

This will involve understanding the principle of markup or gross margin—the difference between the cost of goods sold and the selling price, taking into consideration sale markdowns, shortages and discounts to employees. Generally, markup is stated as a percentage of retail price.

For example, if a manufacturer sells dresses to you at a wholesale price of $12.50 each and you sell them for $25, you would have a 100% markup (a 50% gross margin).

If you know the cost of goods and the average amount of markup you need to operate profitably, it is relatively simple to determine a price by using the following formula:

$$\frac{\text{Cost of goods}}{100 - \text{markup }\%} \times 100 = \text{Retail Price}$$

For example, if you purchased a gross of rubber ducks for a total price of $172.80 and had determined that you needed a gross margin of 36% to operate profitably, you would calculate the expected profit as follows, using the equation above:

$$\frac{\$172.80}{100 - 36} \times 100 = \$270.00$$

When you divide the Retail Price ($270.00) by the number of items (144: a gross) you get a unit price of $1.88, which you would probably raise to $1.98, depending on the market, to improve the profit margin slightly and provide leeway for markdowns during sales, etc.

Specialty items, such as antiques, artwork, imported goods and handcrafted items can be priced higher according to current value and what the market in your area will bear. They generally run between a 200% and 300% markup range.

Setting Wholesale Prices

Operating as a wholesale manufacturer greatly reduces your selling and administrative costs, because you are passing your products on to someone else to sell. Your price to retailers should thus be approximately 50% less than the suggested retail price.

In actuality, you are providing retailers with a discount because of their willingness and ability to promote your product.

The formula for wholesale pricing includes your profit margin + labor costs + expenses, which will be appreciably lower than for a retail operation because of savings on advertising, display equipment and maintenance, but which must include warehousing and marketing.

Pricing is typically more competitive at the wholesale level than at any other and is almost always the determining factor in whether your products are purchased or not.

Also affecting wholesalers are other wholesalers offering competitive pricing, middlemen buying large quantities at low prices and supply and demand factors.

As a wholesaler, you are in a position to vary prices according to the size of orders and your ability to negotiate with buyers. However, it is a good idea to develop a solid markup base from which to operate. This will allow you the flexibility to offer maximum and minimum prices for each item based on quantity buys.

Pricing is a crucial aspect of managing your business. Since you are in business to make a profit, it is important that you set prices that will result in the greatest income.

To do this, you must know what your costs are or, at least, have a solid idea of projected costs if you are still in the process of planning your venture.

By not setting prices that are too high or too low for the product or service you are selling, you will be assured of a favorable position in the market and a healthy share of the wealth.

Inventory as Investment

Ask 100 small business owners what inventory means to them and more than 90% will tell you it's the merchandise they keep on hand to sell to their customers or the materials and supplies stocked to produce goods or perform a service.

This is partially accurate, for inventory can and should be viewed as any supplies, raw materials or finished goods used to generate a profit in your business. But it isn't the response that a savvy business owner would give.

Surprisingly, according to a recent study conducted by a leading consulting firm, less than 10% of a group of 500 entrepreneurs interviewed spoke of their inventory in terms of the investment it represents; an investment that can range from 15% to 25% percent of total operating capital.

> *Although there are countless alumni of the school of hard knocks, there has not yet been a move to accredit that institution.*
>
> *Sonya Rudikoff*

It is because of this "misunderstanding" that many small business owners often fail to incorporate good inventory control practices into their regular management routine. Although they keep an eagle eye on every penny going through the books, they may totally overlook the cash tied up in their inventory.

Controlling Inventory

Inventory control can be a very simple, straightforward task if you implement a workable system from the beginning—preferably even before you start ordering and receiving goods. You will find that time really flies when you are self-employed and it's easy to postpone such tasks as inventory control until, one day, you find yourself facing an overwhelming job.

Inventory control will give you valuable information about: (a) Whether or not you are carrying too much or too little inventory based on, for example, items and prices preferred by your customers, or seasonal aspects, and (b) whether you are realizing optimum economy determined by the costs of storage, taxes, handling and the investment per unit.

The ideal situation is to maintain an inventory that is profitable because it turns over (comes in and goes out of the business) regularly, lowering the cost of storing, displaying and insuring it.

There are several methods of inventory control that you can adopt, depending on your business. The main goal with each method, however, is to tell you how many items you have on hand and how many you need to meet your customer or production demands. It will also work toward lessening inventory shrinkage, which is generally the result of employee pilferage, customer theft, storing inventory incorrectly or maintaining sloppy records of items ordered, received and used.

You can tell how many items you currently have by making an educated guess, which generally works only for businesses having a small, visible inventory that is relatively predictable. An example of the kind of business which could probably operate efficiently with this "relaxed" form of inventory control would be a one- or two-person enterprise that monthly goes through, say, a box of invoices and similar supplies available for a minimum amount at the discount office-supply store.

Other methods of inventory control are the physical count, which should be done at least once a year anyway for tax purposes, or—the easiest and most efficient of them all—maintaining an ongoing record. The best idea is to incorporate the latter two systems—by backing up periodic physical counts with a perpetual record.

To set up your perpetual system, simply create a file card or inventory sheet set up in a three-ring binder for each item in your inventory. Across the top of the card or sheet, list the following:

    a) item name and a code number, if applicable

    b) a description of the item,

    c) where it is stored,

    d) the supplier's name, address and phone number,

    e) unit price (e.g., $12.95/dozen),

    f) your selling price (if a retail item) or percentage of gross price of completed product (if used for manufacturing) or service,

    g) the date you place an order, and

    h) the number of items and the date they are received.

Then, every time you sell or use an item, write it down and subtract it from the last balance. You should also indicate reorder number, based on when and by how much you must replenish your stock. The reorder number will be determined by such factors as: (a) the minimum cost per unit available from your supplier, including quantity discounts, preseason specials and discounts for cash or quick payment, (b) the delivery schedule, from the time you place the order until you receive it, and (c) economic and social trends which can affect the way an item is perceived by the public.

For example, during a period of depressed or inflated

economy, sales for leisure items typically drop. By keeping an eye on these factors, you can adjust your inventory needs accordingly and not get stuck with great quantities of items that you can't move.

After a while, you will be able to recognize at a glance which items are regularly used and which are simply taking up shelf space. When you reach this point, your ordering skills will become much more efficient and your investment in inventory will become a profitable proposition.

16

ORGANIZATION: TIME-MANAGEMENT TIPS

A recent survey of small business owners indicated that one of the qualities they felt contributed the most to their success was organization. In conjunction with this is the fact that time management and basic organizational seminars continue to be the most popular offerings in adult education catalogs and business workshops around the country.

Time is money! Because the small business owner is plagued by a unique set of problems, such as continual interruptions and overworking, it is vital to your success that you learn to manage your time and organize paperwork. This might sound rather simplistic, but you would be amazed at the number of small business owners who operate in a constant state of chaos.

Although we have seen a number of "A messy office is the sign of a creative mind" posters on entrepreneur's office walls, it is a good bet that the holders of these signs can recount story after story of missing checks, lost orders and misplaced files that totally disrupted the flow of business until they were located in a corner pile.

The survey respondents also stated that once they had learned to manage their time in both their personal and business lives and had set up guidelines for handling routine tasks, they felt more confident about accepting new challenges and making decisions.

The simple truth about getting organized is that it clears your mind for taking care of the nitty-gritty, profit-making aspects of being in business—production and promotion. For example, by allotting a certain place in your desk to hold customer files and billing information, you have made one major step toward maximizing production. Knowing that all the needed supplies and materials are located in one spot saves you valuable time and energy.

Making Time Work for You

Time management is the ability to take the hours we have available and use them to our advantage. Making lists of tasks to be done and giving them a priority rating is one of the best ways to avoid losing precious moments.

Keep a monthly calendar handy to help you keep track of major commitments, important dates and appointments. Try to avoid using it for notations of daily work in progress, carry-over tasks or other things that are best suited for inclusion on your daily and weekly lists.

There are several other ideas you can easily incorporate into your working lifestyle that will maximize your productivity.

• Work smart. Handle the jobs you find most difficult or cumbersome during peak performance time. If you are a morning person and find that making telephone calls to potential customers is one of your least favorite responsibilities, take care of them first thing in the morning when you are feeling fresh and energetic, and organize the rest of the day's tasks accordingly.

• Set realistic daily goals for yourself. Just because you are chief cook and bottlewasher, don't try to do everything at once. Learn just how much work you can accept and expect to accomplish in a given period of time and allow yourself to turn down work if it seems as if it will be too much for you to handle.

• Reward yourself. When you are working alone, as many small business owners do when getting their businesses off the ground, there generally aren't many people anywhere around to support or praise your work . . . and everyone needs strokes! While it is true that a customer's praises are an indication that you are doing the right thing, you still need time to relax.

Treat yourself to a special dinner once a week. If money is especially tight, plan an evening where you go to bed early with a good book or do something that has absolutely nothing to do with business. And remind yourself that this is your reward for accomplishing certain goals for the week. It will help to keep your spirits high.

• Don't procrastinate. Don't put off doing tasks that must be done. If you constantly let some tasks slide because you don't enjoy doing them, you will soon find yourself terribly backlogged and unable to catch up. The effects of this may not show themselves until you are faced with a deadline and, at that point, you will discover that you are working at less than maximum efficiency, feeling tense and being hassled by small things. Even when business is slow and it seems that there could be little harm done by taking a day off to visit with a friend, be sure to complete required tasks before closing up shop.

• Limit personal phone calls during established business hours. Personal calls not only eat into productive time, they tie up the line when an important client may be trying to get in touch with you. The same holds true with friendly visitations. If you are self-employed, friends often feel that you are not really "working" and can stop anytime to chat. Explain that you will be happy to visit with them at a specific time and be sure to tell them why, so there aren't any ruffled feathers.

Obviously, there will be times when unavoidable situations, such as an emergency or an unexpected problem, arise. Try to take these inevitabilities into consideration by estimating how long a project will take and then adding a bit of extra time to give yourself leeway.

• Delegate. If you find that you absolutely cannot handle a certain aspect of the business, such as your own bookkeeping, for example, don't labor over the task—you will end up wasting a great deal of time and could make some serious mistakes. Admit to yourself that the task is just not a strong point and have someone else do it.

• Learn to say "No." One of the hardest things for most people to do is to say "no." Even when we realize that, for example, helping a friend out on a special project will eat into valuable time, we often agree to do such things because we hate to say no. What we do is justify our acceptance by assuring ourselves that saying yes will put us in the position of meeting a lot of potential customers. The reality is that using that time to make phone calls or a sales call for your own business will probably result in a paying customer, not just a potential contact.

• Minimize business meetings. Before setting up a formal meeting, which can be very time-consuming, see if you can take care of the matter in question by phone or through the mail. If a meeting can't be avoided, make sure you specify a time limit to encourage people to get down to business. Another time-saving device for meetings is to work up an agenda that outlines exactly what has to be discussed to avoid idle chit-chat and unnecessary diversions.

• Plan your time. When you have to run errands, plan them for a time that is most convenient, such as in the morning when traffic is light. Plan to do as many things as possible in one trip, outlining the stops you must make so they follow a sequential order.

17

OPERATIONS:
7 STEPS FOR LINGERIE SUCCESS

There will be many variables as to how you decide to start, manage and run your lingerie business—location, personnel, suppliers, advertising—some of which you'll have to rely on your good common sense. There are, however, basic plans of attack to ensure your success and growth in the mail order lingerie world.

These seven steps outline a good way to organize and plan your operations process. Some of these steps might need rearranging due to unforeseen needs that your particular lingerie business will encounter. The order of these steps is important, but not set in stone. After doing your critical research and reviewing the options at hand, you'll be able to arrange this outline in the most beneficial way.

1. Focusing the Business

Now knowing what it takes to start your lingerie mail order company, where do you feel you should focus the business? Are you willing and able to provide a broad selection of lingerie or do you feel that in your market you should specialize?

Answering these questions will be the first step in organizing and planning your lingerie venture. Most start-up companies will specialize in a specific area and then expand as the business grows and demand warrants.

Areas of lingerie specialization can be determined by three factors: item, size or style. Specializing by item is one way to focus your business. Starting a "panties only" mail order company in which you carry a wide range of sizes, styles and colors of panties only could be perfect for your market and start-up goals.

Basing the company on particular sizes is another lucrative solution. There is a very large market for "petites only" or for "full-figured" or other size-based buyers. Offering a particular range of sizes can narrow your initial capital investment and concentrate your efforts.

Third, focusing the business on one particular style or material can also help benefit your start-up. "Purely silk" or "lace only" might be two particular avenues on which you might want to concentrate. Whichever way you decide to go in the beginning, remember that you can always expand later and increase the number of items, sizes and/or styles.

2. Naming the Business

It's very important that you decide on a name for your mail order lingerie business and file the proper forms and records. Legally, your company will exist as a business entity allowing you to make money, but more important, having a solid name will have psychological weight with any supplier, company or contact that you deal with.

When you start calling suppliers to get prices, you're going to have to present yourself professionally. Calling a national lingerie manufacturer and saying, "I'm thinking of starting a mail order business and need to get some prices and information" probably won't get you as far as you need to go. Calling and saying, "Hello, this is Mary Ardmore, president of Ardmore Lingerie Sales. I'm looking for new lingerie and undergarment suppliers and would like to get some price information..." should get you everything you need. It makes you sound and feel more professional.

After you've decided where to focus the business, a name should come to you quickly. In this industry a lot of companies use the owner's name like Darla Sharpe Lingerie or Shirley of Hollywood. Others prefer to capitalize on the product or concept like Global Bra Supplies or National Lingerie Wholesalers.

It's also important to have tangible backup as far as your business is concerned. Printed business cards and letterhead will further your presence when you have to contact businesses through the mail or when suppliers or retailers request information from you.

3. The Supply Line

Obviously you need to have products to sell, but up to this point you probably have only a passing idea as to what they'll cost or where to get them. Locating suppliers and having a price and availability work-up on each of them is your next step.

In the Resources section at the end of this book, we've supplied you with a list of national lingerie, undergarment, and apparel suppliers, manufacturers and wholesalers. It may seem like a substantial list, but there are many more out there.

Looking for suppliers will be like shopping for a car or a new TV set. You're going to want to first find the right person to talk to (usually the sales or wholesale manager—whoever can make the best deal) and get all the pertinent information about their operation, prices, availability and delivery. Some key questions and their reasons will be:

What quantity discounts do you offer? (Buying in bulk will reduce your costs overall.)

What are your shipping charges? (The product costs might be low but with the shipping costs added, you might be paying too much.)

Is shipping free if I order a specific amount of any product? (Along with quantity discounts, some manufacturers will give you a break on shipping at certain amounts.)

Do you have any warehouses nearby? (Some manufacturers have strategically placed warehouses throughout the U.S. One might be in your town, saving you time and shipping costs.)

How soon do you ship after the order is placed? (Time is of the essence; if you have to wait, your customers will have to wait.)

Do you offer credit accounts/what are your terms? (By having 30, 60 or 90 days in which to pay for inventory, you can have revenue pay for product as opposed to cash up front. This will ease cash flow tremendously.)

Will your company drop ship? (Many wholesalers and manufacturers will give you the option of drop shipping at a price. If this price is less than what you'd pay to fulfill orders yourself—shipping supplies, personnel, time, shipping costs—this is the best option.)

What is the charge for drop shipping? (Get all the costs before you decide.)

Do you offer preprinted catalogs to your resellers? (Quite a few wholesalers and manufacturers produce their own professional product catalogs, whereby you pay to have your business name printed on each one that you send out. This will save you the added time and expense of producing your own.)

Do you offer product shots and copy for resellers' catalogs? (If the wholesalers and manufacturers don't supply catalogs they should have sell copy and product shots that you can use in the catalogs or brochures that you produce. This will save you the time and expense of writing and photography.)

Why should I use your company over a competitor's? (The mere mention of a competitor informs the supplier that you are looking for the best deal. Usually they'll get to the bottom line sooner and explain in exact terms what makes their products and services better.)

What other non-lingerie or related products do you supply? (When time comes to expand the business, knowing that an established supplier has the products you're looking for will make it that much easier.)

Again, depending on the focus of your lingerie company, these questions might need to be tailored to your specific needs. Your ultimate goals are quality with affordability and availability.

4. Your Marketing Mix

How will you present your company and its products and services to the buying public? How involved will your catalog, brochure or flyers be? Are you reaching a large enough audience with these promotional pieces?

You should be asking and answering as many of these questions as possible. This stage is vital. You should know at least some of the basics for your marketing and advertising by now: what your target region is (local, county-wide, statewide, regional or national), how big the market is (population of consumers) and how you'll be reaching them (catalog, brochure, flyers, or other means).

You now need to concentrate on how your message will be getting to the general public. Have you contacted a mailing list broker for possible lists of lingerie buyers? Are you ready to send out promotional material outlining your new business and what you're offering? You've researched costs and timing on producing a catalog or a brochure. Can you afford it right now? If you can't, have you thought of any other options?

Producing a catalog has been highly emphasized throughout this guide, but don't despair if it's outside your budget right now. There are other options that can get you started building your lingerie business:

Space advertising – putting together a display ad for regional newspapers or magazines is one way of bypassing the catalog route in the beginning.

A **display ad** designed with as many good product shots and prices as possible, placed in high subscriber or volume newspapers or periodicals (in the region you're marketing) can work quite well. A consumer can see what he or she wants and order directly, provided your pricing and professional appearance compete with other retail advertisers. This may not work as well as a direct mail catalog, but should lower your advertising costs substantially and start you building a good local client base.

Home parties – there is a definite tongue-in-cheek response when anyone mentions Tupperware parties, those get-togethers where people would visit a neighbor's house for cocktails and appetizers and have the virtues of Tupperware extolled upon them. Even during their heyday in the '50s and '60s it wasn't for everyone—to host or participate in. But ask any of the enterprising house-

Ring-necked Pheasant

EASTBAY BRIDAL
REESHEMAH O MCCULLOUGH
7877 OUTLOOK AVE
OAKLAND, CA 94605

23

wives or couples who made a mint doing it how often they chuckled all the way to the bank!

This home party idea has translated very well to the lingerie industry. By capitalizing on the privacy and home-based aspect that expands lingerie sales, home parties are quickly becoming an excellent way to start a mail order lingerie business.

Contact family, friends and neighbors with a flyer or phone call telling them about the next lingerie party you're having. Make sure you have a decent supply of products on hand for participants to see, compare and try on. You may want to have enough stock to sell right then and there or supply order forms so each product can be delivered or shipped. (This can further reduce your initial inventory costs by ordering from your supplier only what's been sold.) Fame Time (see Resources) produces a helpful booklet on intimate home lingerie parties that will detail some of the ways you can capitalize on this type of marketing.

Other marketing means – you will probably come up with other ways to sell your lingerie and other methods of marketing that will work very well. One thing you'll learn is that what works for others may not work for you—and vice versa. It will take a little time and testing to find the right mix for your unique mail order lingerie business. Don't get discouraged–a little perseverance will profit a long way.

5. Processing Orders

You've found the best suppliers; you've got the inventory taken care of; you're advertising in newspapers and sending out catalogs. But how are you processing your orders? When your response hits like a tidal wave, are you going to be able to handle it? What kind of backup plans do you have?

Based on your marketing projections, you have a

rough idea of how many orders you'll be processing on a regular basis. Have you decided on whether your catalog order form and display advertising will make buyers respond directly to your business address, P.O. Box, business phone number or a combination of the three? Have you looked for an answering service in your area that can supply you with an 800 number and operators 24 hours a day, should your response overwhelm you?

If you've calculated how much time it will take from the point of receiving an order to shipping the product out the door, and then multiplied that by the number of orders you think you'll be getting, you know how much of your day will be spent processing orders. Can you alone handle this flow without sacrificing your promised product delivery time? Can you meet these deadlines while performing all the other business tasks that need to be done on any given day? Do you have family or friends willing to help out on immediate notice or will you hire the help?

More to the point, how exactly does your fulfillment process take place? You should have a very precise way of organizing the overall task for processing orders. First list every function involved and see what each task entails as far as time and energy. A standard mail order lingerie operation should function generally in this order:

1. Order Entry (Caging and Cashiering)

When you receive and group all orders for a specific day or time period (caging), the money functions (cashiering—processing cash, checks, money orders and credit card info, entering the order data, generating a receipt or invoice) should be separated from the order fulfillment side of the business (gathering the products, packaging, labeling and shipping). Process the order by entering the customer's data, product requests and payment method into your record-keeping system. (You can manually record orders in a ledger and write out receipts, but using a computer and specific invoicing software will handle this task much more quickly and efficiently.)

What kinds of funds will you accept? Most people won't send cash through the mail and it can be a hazard when you've got employees opening the orders without supervision. Money orders made out to your company are treated the same as cash, but can be redeemed only by you. Checks are the second most used form of paying for mail order items. The only problems you'll encounter will be for the wrong amounts written on the checks or that the customer's account is overdrawn and the check is no good. Most mail order companies have a longer delay for sending out an order that was purchased by check. This gives the bank time to process the check and clear it as being okay. If you're going to honor personal checks, you may want to set up your own policy for shipping delay.

For mail order, the ease of using a credit card is one of the fundamental factors that has helped its growth over the last decade. People purchase more easily now that most major credit card companies will protect against fraud or lost items—making it the best option for you.

When you've set up your checking and perhaps savings accounts at the bank, ask about obtaining a credit card acceptance kit. It should include the proper forms and information about the requirements and operations for each vendor (i.e., Visa, MasterCard, American Express).

All moneys should be collected, recorded, then deposited (for cash, checks or money orders) or verified (for credit cards). Once payment has been verified and deposited, you're under obligation to fulfill an order within 30 days by law.

CODs (Cash On Delivery) used to be popular with mail order companies because of the speed in which an order could be fulfilled. Nowadays due to risk, package tracking problems and general criminality and fraud, most companies won't send products COD. It can still be used; however, we don't recommend it.

Generate an invoice or receipt listing the products ordered and pass this along to the fulfillment side of the business.

2. Gathering Product and Packaging

Once you've caged and cashiered, you need to gather the customer's products and package them for shipment. It's hoped that you've set up a good inventory system where all products are sorted in bins and labeled—making gathering a snap. Or you've arranged to send bulk orders to your supplier and have them send you the product immediately or drop-ship the product directly to the customer. Either way, this step can add a lot of time to the fulfillment process if not planned carefully from the beginning.

After gathering the products for an order, place them neatly inside the package along with the receipt/invoice and perhaps a "bounce-back" catalog or coupon for the customer's next order (once a customer, always a customer as the saying goes). Your packaging should be sturdy enough to handle the rigors of shipping without damaging the products inside. Luckily, lingerie isn't that fragile; your main concern will be keeping it clean if the bag or box should open or split.

3. Generating Labels and Shipping

No matter which carrier you use (USPS Express Mail, FedEx, UPS, Airborne Express, etc.) you'll need to fill out separate forms for shipping each of your packages and produce address labels to attach to each one. This can become quite time consuming if done manually. Again, your computer can come to your rescue. Shipping software that will automatically fill out Federal Express and UPS forms, along with generating labels from your order entry/invoicing software, is available for usually less than $60 (see Resources section for info).

You should also have an account set up with your carrier so they can bill you on a regular basis. This will save you the time and hassle of writing checks and figuring shipping costs daily. And just because these are big companies you're dealing with, don't underestimate their willingness to bargain. Many mail order companies get sizable volume discounts based on their shipping quantities. Find out what volume you need to be shipping to qualify for savings.

All forms generated from shipping need to be filed and readily accessed should there be a customer who doesn't receive his or her package or receives one that's damaged. It will be up to you to provide the shipping number and information should these types of problems arise.

6. Restocking and Inventory Control

By now you know what's selling. You know what you ran out of and had to reorder at the last minute. You know what didn't sell a single unit. You know what products take up the most room, and you know how long it takes to get specific items. Staying on top of your restocking is what's known as inventory control.

Inventory control will be a growing concern as your business expands. Keeping the in-demand products moving quickly and not accumulating a lot of poor sellers will be the basic trick; and now that you have a good idea of what kind of response you're getting for certain items, you can order accordingly.

You'll start seeing trends in what people are buying based on season, or style, or functionality or almost anything else. Orders for some items will start to drop while other things that weren't selling really take off. Controlling your purchasing by watching these trends through your orders will be a unique experience. No other company will be witnessing the shifts in demand exactly like yours, making this part of the business unique. Granted there will be general occurrences affecting all lingerie companies—heatwaves reducing the demand for flannel boxers, a silk shortage driving the prices for designer bras up, or a change in style that makes animal print items all the rage again—but only you will be able to best predict your inventory flow.

As things change, always keep an eye out for a better supplier or better ways to reduce your inventory and product costs. Stay abreast of current industry developments in manufacturing, product supply and materials by joining some of the associations listed at the end of this business guide.

7. Remarketing

Just as you're looking for newer and better suppliers, you should always be looking for newer and better ways to market your lingerie business and build your client base. Watch what the competition is doing—where they're mailing, what lists they're renting, how their catalogs are arranged, etc. A lot of tried-and-true methods of promotion and advertising are in use that work; don't knock yourself out trying to do something brand new or unique; stick with what works and keep improving it.

Keep a list of potential buyers that might have requested a catalog or information recently but didn't purchase anything. If they were interested once, they'll be interested again. People buy lingerie differently; sometimes they need an extra little push. It could be a 10% discount offer for first time buyers or a "buy-one-get-one-free" deal. Keep a record of the promotions that work for you and routinely rotate them and test new ideas. This will build your business and give it the mark of professionalism.

Producing Your Catalog

At some point on your path to success in mail order lingerie, you'll no doubt need to produce your own product catalog. For the novice, this can become a daunting task—

coordinating products, models, photographers, designers, printers—and can end up costing more than you might have planned for.

This section will outline the process of putting together a basic, 16 page, color catalog, explaining many of the design and printing terms along with shortcuts and cost saving information.

Catalog vs. Brochure

Thanks to advances in technology, most common brochures are now produced "in-house" using a computer and laser printer to make solid, functional information pieces. They are usually printed on standard 8.5 inch x 11 inch paper, folded in half and stapled, containing product information and line art pictures. They can be as inexpensive as 1¢ a piece to produce and provide the basic information for product orders.

For local, or regional marketing, well done in-house brochures can function quite well, keeping overall costs to a minimum with the ability to alter and reprint on a moment's notice.

But, as is the case, low cost means low excitement—many buyers are used to full color photography and glossy paper bursting with "sell-copy" promoting sales and new products. This is what makes a catalog more apt to produce the desired sales response than that of a brochure.

Step 1 - Figuring the Size

First off, you need to decide how big (number of pages, size of catalog, number of copies to print) you want your catalog to be. The size of the catalog will depend on the money you have available and the number of catalogs you need to produce. It might sound like a "chicken-or-the-egg" scenario—how do you know how big a catalog you can produce if you don't how much it will cost?—but read through all these steps before finalizing any one plan of action.

You'll hope you've looked at as much of the competition's materials as possible (catalogs, mailings, promotions) and have a better understanding of what needs to be accomplished. A good way to proceed is to treat each page of your catalog as "shelf space" like in a retail or grocery store. You have a limited amount of space in which to showcase your products and you want to maximize your ROI (return on investment). This can best be accomplished by continuous testing (measuring the response—the number of orders—for each product based on the amount of space it occupies in your catalog). It's a fact that the more space you give a product, the better it will sell and the more profit can be generated. However, there reaches a point at which the profit starts to drop off when the space used gets too large. This is called the point of diminishing returns. Through testing, you'll know the point of diminishing returns for each product you sell—fully maximizing your profit for each catalog you send out.

Set up two plans for your catalog: what you'd prefer to have (72+ pages, full color, modeled products, glossy cover) and what you can get by with (32 pages, black and white with a color "cover wrap," product only shots and line art). You'll find there are many, many options to producing a catalog; some things you'll definitely want and others you could live without. As you proceed through the catalog production process, gaining a better understanding of the options, you'll be able to decide what those characteristics are.

For each plan, gather the pertinent information:

How many products do you/will you offer?

How large is your customer base (number of people in the region or mailing list you're using)?

How many of these products will benefit greatly from being shown in color?

> Which of your suppliers have products shots or
>   line art drawings already available?
> Have you looked at how other lingerie catalogs
>   are presented?
> Of those, which are more attractive or catch
>   your attention more?
> How large are they (both by dimension and
>   page count)?
> How do they arrange (layout) the products on
>   each page?
> What is the overall order of products throughout
>   these catalogs?
> Which ideas would you like to incorporate into
>   your design?
> Which ones don't you like?
> How heavy or glossy is the paper used in these
>   catalogs?
> Is there a separate cover wrap?
> Is it bound (with a spine like a book) or is it stapled?
> Which would you prefer?

Compare and contrast, then note what you prefer and what you think you can get by with (without sacrificing your professional look and appeal).

Step 2 - Getting the Printing Costs

Next to mailing, printing is where you're going to see substantial costs. You should have both of your catalog preferences outlined with notes on the items that you really want and those you don't. You should at this point (if you haven't already) contact the Printing Industries Association (see Resources/Printing) for a list of printers able to handle your catalog job.

When contacting a printer, you'll usually want to talk to a salesperson. They will take all the information from you, ask you about the specifics of your catalog, and usually offer advice on how to print it the most cost effective way (this is generally referred to as "bidding the job"). They, in turn, pass this information on to their estimator (a person who calculates how soon your job could be printed, how long it will take to print, and how much your job will cost). Just as you've shopped around for lingerie suppliers, it will benefit you greatly to shop around for printers—you'll be surprised at the range of costs and the amount you can save finding the right one.

Another thing to keep in mind is your shipping cost. A printer will generally quote you a production price—without shipping charges included. As you can tell, finding a nearby printer will save you money in this area. Either way, find out what the charges are and if there are any other "hidden" costs not included in the bid.

Step 3 - Gathering Copy

By now, you've got a price range for your catalog printing. You've decided on the quantity you're going to print and the catalog makeup (number of pages, color or black and white, cover wrap, etc.)—based on what your printer has suggested and what you really want. Because of this, you now must decide which of your products you'll be featuring, what order they'll be in, and how your catalog will look.

Have your suppliers provided you with any product photographs or line art? Have you asked them? By gathering as much of the art work from your suppliers as possible, you can greatly reduce the cost of producing them yourself.

If you have to supply your own product pictures, you can hire a photographer or photograph them yourself. Obviously, taking the pictures yourself will reduce the expense, but you might be sacrificing quality if you're an amateur photographer. You might want to hire a photographer to shoot your cover photo and a few of the key products you'll be promoting while you handle the rest. Also keep in mind that in a lot of instances you won't need a product photo at all—a good, detailed description can help you there.

As far as product descriptions go, you can no doubt write these yourself. You know which products are hot sellers, what materials are used, how they fit, how attractive they look and so on. This is your business and you know what you're selling. This will save you the expense of hiring a professional writer who may not understand how you want to promote your lingerie in your catalog.

Step 4 - Laying Out/Designing the Catalog

Once you've gathered all the copy (photos, line art, descriptions) you'll need to lay them out in an organized and calculated matter. Think back to your research of the competition's position of products. They no doubt have calculated their points of diminishing returns and will be good models for your initial layout.

For this exercise, we'll say our catalog is going to be 16 pages long and is 5.5 inches x 8.5 inches (8 standard 8.5 inch x 11 inch sheets folded in half).

Start by using blank sheets of regular white bond paper folded in half (like a catalog) and numbered from 1 to 16. At this point you can start rough-sketching in products in the best manner you see fit. Maybe the first four pages are bras only, the next four are panties and slips, two pages of teddies, four pages of chemises, and the last two have miscellaneous other products—however you've decided based on your calculated profitability and competition research.

You don't have to be a good artist to sketch in your layout. Just use basic squares or shapes for photos and descriptions, and write in the product number or name. Another more precise way to arrange your catalog is by photocopying items (reducing and enlarging where needed), and cutting them out and pasting them in the positions you want. This will give you a better visual idea of how your catalog will look and help along the prepress (all the functions involved in getting a catalog ready to be printed) stages of your printing.

Step 5 - Final Production

It's at this point you might need to hire a graphic designer or production artist to translate your layout and ideas into a format that the printer can use to print your catalog. Nowadays this process is done almost entirely (and much more cost effectively) on a computer. You could purchase the correct software programs to do the job, but the time and energy involved in learning to use it would far outweigh the one time cost of hiring someone.

Many graphic designers or production artists can be found in the phone book or by contacting the GATF (Graphic Arts Technical Foundation in the Resource section) for a list of acceptable artists in your area. Because of the nature of graphic design and the number of artists nowadays, the price per hour has dropped significantly. When interviewing a potential designer, ask for references and samples of work relating to catalog production—you in turn will supply much of the information you gave to the printer in Step 2.

Once you've selected a production artist, explain all the ideas and wants you require for your catalog—overall look, feel, emphasis and color. You will also want to provide him or her with the proper specifications for how the printer wants your final production work (this should have been provided from your information in Step 2 also—if not, ask). It will be the production artist's responsibility to provide you with the finished art, ready for print, in the exact form requested.

Step 6 - Printing and Proofing

When you submit your final artwork to the printer, he or she in turn will prepare it for the printing press and supply you with a set of blue lines (or brown lines as they are sometimes referred to) for you to give your final approval on. These are usually single color (blue, gray or brown) pages showing you exactly what will be printed once the job starts. It's vital at this point to check everything—placement of photos, page numbers, misspellings, crooked art—and report any problems to the printer. What you see will be what you get, and you don't want what you get to be wrong! You've put so much energy into making your catalog a success, don't make a mistake at this point.

A good rule of thumb is to go through the catalog three times. Once as a casual, interested reader (much like your customers will), second as a visual inspector (checking that all graphic elements are okay) and finally as a copy editor (reading every word and checking every headline and product name). Have a friend or employee read through it also to spot any items you might have missed— just to be sure!

All's Well That Tests Well

Soon you will have your final, professional catalog in your hand, ready to send out and bring the orders flooding in. You'll also have your first set of good data on each product to use for future catalogs and tests—did some products sell better than others? What if you rearrange the order of products? Change the size of each picture? Use more descriptive copy? Use less? How will all of these changes affect sales...? All the questions will form the basis of your continued trials of bettering your profit and minimizing your costs. It's the main secret in guaranteeing mail order lingerie—or any other product business—a success!

Expanding the Business

As you no doubt can tell, there are plenty of opportunities to expand your mail order lingerie operation. You've seen how Victoria's Secret is following the conservative path and branching out into more basic women's clothing and how Frederick's of Hollywood covers the more exotic and sensual market.

Since your business focus is based on one of the three basic market niches (the functional buyer, the exotic buyer, and the comfort buyer) along with one of the three specialized areas (specific items, specific sizes, or specific styles), it shouldn't be too hard to see where you should expand. You've been tracking special orders and customer requests, which should tell you where a lot of your buyers would like to see your business grow.

Try testing a few new products in your next catalog, brochure or display ad. You may want to start expanding by carrying a larger range of sizes, items or styles. If you were a "bras only" company you might try adding panties, hosiery or slips. If you were "full-figured sizes only" you might increase your range to include standard sizes and petites. If you've been successful selling "cotton only" lingerie and you've seen an increase in silk or chiffon demand, go in that direction. As with a lot of the mail order lingerie processes, you will be encountering unique situations. Use your experience and common sense to make prudent decisions about your business's future.

Follow the Leaders

The most common areas for expansion that we've seen from our research have been in the areas that tie in well with the concepts of mail order lingerie—the privacy and anonymity factors, wider selections than retail outlets, as well as better ranges of sizes, styles and availability.

At the top of the list is sleepwear. Nightgowns, night-shirts, silk undershirts, pajamas and long johns, to name a few items, go well with lingerie and naturally fit in a lingerie catalog. Many of your suppliers probably already offer many of these garments and can supply you right away. If they don't, they will probably know who does.

Also rating high and fitting right in with lingerie is swimwear. Many customers who want the privacy of buying lingerie at home feel the same way about swimwear—bikinis, g-strings, one-pieces. Again, many of the manu-facturers and wholesalers you're dealing with also sell or can provide swimwear. Bali Company, for example, deals almost entirely with just lingerie and swimwear—finding that perfect match in the marketplace and supplying it to you.

> *Knowledge is of two kinds. We know a subject our-selves or we know where we can find information on it.*
>
> *Samuel Johnson*

Bath accessories, per-fumes and lotions are natural compliments to lingerie. Fragrant soaps, bath gels, designer perfumes and body lotions stimulate the senses much in the same way lingerie does. Providing both together will definitely expand your profitability in the right direction.

If you're noticing that many of your customers are ordering lingerie that is of the erotic and seductive nature, you may consider selling products that fall within the "marital aid" category. These items are designed primarily to enhance relationships, sensuality and love-making. They include books, costumes, toys, videos and accessories that many consumers purchase regularly. Some might consider this area too risque or consider it "pornographic" in nature, but there are many legitimate and respectable items that fall into this category. If this is something you might be interested in, our advice is to first look through a sensual product catalog like The Xandria Gold Edition Catalog (see Resources) and decide if these are items that would fit in with your lingerie selection—many of them should, and offer you an excellent additional income stream.

18

PERSONNEL: HIRING EMPLOYEES

As your lingerie business gets going, you'll quickly realize that there aren't enough hours in the day to get everything done. You've budgeted your time well, but you're starting to fall behind. You know how much time the order processing and fulfillment part alone can take up. And once your order demand really gets going, you will need to consider hiring an employee to help with the workload and give you the opportunity to recruit new business. Although your profit margin will be higher if you do it all alone, when business reaches the point where you are not able to handle all the orders in addition to maintaining the business, it's time to get help. This might come rather soon in your mail order lingerie business.

You can begin by getting someone on a part-time basis. That person may be interested in working full-time when the need arises; a situation you can play by ear. In the meantime, you know that for a certain number of hours per day or per week, someone else will be there to do those things you are simply too busy to get to—entering orders, making bank deposits, sorting lingerie into the boxes, and generating shipping labels. The idea is to keep the customer happy and to get the products out in a timely fashion, and if this means hiring another person, that's what you do.

When the time comes for you to hire an employee or two for your business, you will want the most suitable people you can find. It is important to know what you are looking for in terms of personnel before you start the recruiting and interviewing process. For mail order lingerie, someone with good data entry skills, organization, computer experience and a general interest in the undergarment industry would be an ideal candidate.

Selecting Candidates

Have interested applicants fill out a standard employment application (as shown on the following pages) and provide references from former employers and business associates. Do not just take the information provided at face value; check these references very carefully to find out about the applicant's sense of loyalty, responsibility and honesty. This can be done by phone or with a letter.

In either case, request answers to specific questions dealing with those factors that are most important to your job requirements; in this case promptness, character and courtesy, dependability, work habits and loyalty. Be wary of candidates who list friends or relatives as references; they could be trying to conceal unfavorable information.

The Janson Co.
34659 Virginia Road
Anytown, USA 94635

Please Print

As an equal opportunity employer, our company policy as well as federal, state, and city laws, prohibits discrimination in employment based on race, color, religion, sex, national origin, age, or physical handicaps unrelated to job performance.

General

NAME	Last	First	Middle		SOCIAL SECURITY NUMBER

PRESENT ADDRESS	Street	City	State	Zip	TELEPHONE NUMBER	EMERGENCY NO.

PREVIOUS ADDRESS	Street	City	State	Zip	LENGTH OF TIME AT ADDRESS

POSITION DESIRED

SCHEDULE PREFERRED
FULL-TIME ☐   PART-TIME ☐

Are you related to anyone employed by this company?

YES ☐   NO ☐

REFERRED BY

Name _____

DATE AVAILABLE

Relationship _____

SALARY DESIRED
$

Position _____

Employment History (Most Recent Employer First)

EMPLOYMENT	NAME AND ADDRESS OF EMPLOYER	POSITION/RESPONSIBILITIES
FROM		
TO	SUPERVISOR TELEPHONE NO.	
SALARY	REASON FOR LEAVING	
FROM		
TO	SUPERVISOR TELEPHONE NO.	
SALARY	REASON FOR LEAVING	
FROM		
TO	SUPERVISOR TELEPHONE NO.	
SALARY	REASON FOR LEAVING	

Education

	NAME AND ADDRESS	NO. OF YEARS	YEAR GRAD.	SUBJECTS STUDIED
HIGH SCHOOL				
TRADE OR BUSINESS SCHOOL				
COLLEGE OR UNIVERSITY				
OTHER				

FOREIGN LANGUAGES SPOKEN

References (List the names of three persons not related to you.)

NAME & ADDRESS	JOB TITLE	YRS. KNOWN	TELEPHONE

Skills (Check the applicable areas in which you have experience.)

☐ TYPING
WORDS PER MINUTE _____

☐ WORD PROCESSING
☐ DATA PROCESSING

☐ SPREADSHEET
☐ 10-KEY ADDING MACH.

☐ EPBX, PBX
☐ DICTAPHONE

LIST APPLICABLE
SOFTWARE PACKAGES:

WORD PROCESSING _____
DATA PROCESSING _____

SPREADSHEET _____
GRAPHIC _____

CHECK COMPUTER SYSTEMS WITH
WHICH YOU'RE EXPERIENCED:

☐ IBM
☐ IBM-COMPATIBLES

☐ MACINTOSH
☐ OTHER _____

LIST OTHER SKILLS YOU POSSESS:

Additional Information

HAVE YOU EVER SERVED IN THE UNITED STATES ARMED FORCES? ☐ NO ☐ YES
If yes, give years of service and final rank:

HAVE YOU EVER BEEN CONVICTED OF A FELONY OR A MISDEMEANOR? ☐ NO ☐ YES
If yes, explain in detail:

I certify that all information provided on this application is correct to the best of my knowledge. I understand that willful omission or deliberate falsification of this information is grounds for termination.

APPLICANT'S SIGNATURE: _____   DATE: _____

The Janson Co.
34659 Virginia Road
Anytown USA 94635

Joan Anderson
Staffing & Employment Department
34659 Virginia Road
Anytown, USA 94635

Dear Applicant:

Thank you for applying for a position with the Janson Co. We welcome your interest in our organization.

We continually evaluate candidates' backgrounds and interests against our current personnel requirements. Be assured we'll review your experience and you'll be notified within 10 working days if your qualifications appear to meet our current needs. If there is not a current match, your application will be kept in our files and reviewed as future openings occur.

Again, thank you for your interest in the Janson Co.

Sincerely,

Joan Anderson

Joan Anderson
Staffing Administrator

The Interview Process

Schedule a personal interview to make your own determination based on poise, appearance, level of interest in the job, abilities and future goals. Write out any questions you may have ahead of time to help you stay on track.

Set up the interview in a comfortable place to put the candidate at ease. For example, if you operate out of your home, arrange to meet at a convenient location during a slow time, or if you have an office, set it up when you won't be bombarded by phone calls or people stopping in. In addition to finding out about their capabilities and goals, you will want to use this time to talk about the company, your expectations, standards and, of course, the pay structure. In this case you might also want to devise a simple test related to the candidate's knowledge of the job.

On-the-Job Training

When you find someone who seems to have all the qualifications needed, arrange to train him or her on the job. Many owners like to do this themselves, to ensure that their standards are instilled from the beginning and to get a first-hand idea of the new recruit's work habits.

If you have a trusted employee on staff, have the new recruit accompany him or her on assignments to learn the ropes. This extra duty should always result in a bonus for the employee doing the training.

Training may take several weeks or months, depending on the worker's previous experience. Basically, a good training process should involve the following steps:

- Gain the recruit's confidence by putting him or her at ease.
- Find out what he or she already knows.
- Indicate the importance of each aspect of brokering a deal.
- Explain and show each step patiently.

- Be sure each step is understood before moving on to another.
- Encourage and welcome questions.
- Have the recruit try to do the task.
- Correct mistakes gently.
- Have him or her repeat the steps to you.
- When you are both comfortable, let the recruit go out alone.
- Review performance periodically.
- Offer support by letting the employee train others when ready.

Taking time to train properly reduces turnover, improves the quality of work performed and, in addition, lowers your cost of labor.

Overtraining the Ambitious

Sometimes, it is possible to train people so well they feel they can start their own business in competition with yours. This occasionally happens when an employee realizes you are making money off his or her hard work. There are several ways to stay on top of your employees' activity.

If you're certain an employee is thinking of starting his or her own business, take him or her aside and explain the administrative aspects of the business. Find out if they truly realize what you are doing for them in terms of finding work on a continual basis and if they understand how much is involved in running their own business.

In rare cases, you are going to lose an employee who feels confident enough to start his or her own business, and there isn't too much you can do about it.

In other situations, you can "promote" the employee by making him or her a "senior executive" or sales manager, as appropriate. This is feasible only if your cash flow and the employee's ability warrant it.

The Benefits of Happy Employees

Personnel management is a time-consuming job for business owners. However, paying attention to the needs of your employees and working to gain their trust and maintain loyalty can do nothing but benefit your business.

The attitude of your employees about your management techniques plays an important part in building and maintaining your reputation in the community.

If employees are treated fairly and with respect, their job satisfaction will be reflected in the way they do their job.

This is something that can truly keep you ahead of the competition; a loyal, efficient and enthusiastic group of workers is one of your most effective forms of public relations, so never scrimp when it comes to keeping your employees happy. A few important rules of thumb in dealing with employees include the following:

• Never expect an employee to do something that you wouldn't do. This is why training new recruits yourself is such a good idea; it shows them that you are willing and able to step in and do anything required if necessary.

• Listen to your employees and incorporate their ideas whenever it is feasible. Suggestions that work for the good of the company should be rewarded with a bonus.

• Take the time to talk about business standards and practices so that everyone knows exactly what is expected of them. Outline duties and responsibilities on the job and schedule regular reviews to ensure that they are constantly met. If you find it necessary to talk to any employees about their work habits, do it in private so they are not embarrassed in front of their peers. And do not criticize; merely offer constructive ways that they can improve their performance.

• Treat each employee as an individual. When someone seems to be having personal problems that are interfering with his or her ability to work, be willing to allow the person time off without penalty to take care of the situation. An employee plagued with problems may carry them into the client's home or to the event site and this would have a negative effect. It is much better to get someone to fill in until the regular employee is operating at full efficiency again.

• If a particular client is having a personality conflict with an employee, assure the employee that it isn't his or her fault and point out the benefits to everyone involved of sending in a replacement.

19

ADVERTISING YOUR BUSINESS

More than 150 years ago, Thomas Macaulay, a British historian and statesman, said, "Advertising is to business what steam is to industry. [They provide] the same propelling power."

Few in business would argue with Macaulay's observation—it is as true today as it was when steam was the driving force behind industry. But the question remains, "How do you get the most out of your advertising dollar?" The answer is to (a) know your customer, (b) target your market, and (c) understand the basics of advertising.

This section discusses the various aspects of advertising, including how to use circulation figures to figure your cost per thousand (CPM) and how to create ads that will bring results.

What Is Advertising?

Advertising informs the public about:
• Who you are,
• What kind of business you operate,
• How they can buy your products or services, and
• Why they should come to you.

Before you even open the doors of your business, you should start thinking about your advertising program—how much money you can afford to spend, where your dollars will be best spent and how to structure your campaign.

Decide what kind of results you expect. Are you looking for immediate sales or ongoing recognition? What kind of customers are you hoping to attract? Are you emphasizing price, service, workmanship or something unique? Once you have answered these questions, your decision as to the best type of advertising for the allotted dollars will be easier to make.

There are three basic types of advertising that you will be most interested in during the first few years of your business.

Start-up Advertising: This includes your business cards and stationery, the flyers and brochures you have created to announce your new business, and your initial newspaper advertising campaign. Your main focus here will be on telling people where you are located and what you can offer them.

Ongoing Advertising: Once the business is "up and running," so to speak, it will be vital to your success to institute a regular advertising campaign that is well-planned and, this is the key, consistent. Your goal, at this point, is to attract new clients, obtain repeat business from existing clients, and enhance your reputation.

Looking Good: After you have reached the point where your business is on steady ground and showing increased profits every year, you can afford to dabble in "institutional advertising," as it is called in the trade. This is where you pick up the tab to send a dozen kids to the rodeo when it comes to town or sponsor a float in the local Fourth of July parade and, in return, get your name listed on the program or on a banner in the parade. This is primarily name recognition only and, while every little bit is helpful, by the time you can afford it, you probably will be in pretty good shape anyway.

Yellow Pages

Few successful operators claim that they can build their businesses strictly by word-of-mouth referrals. If you're planning to structure a full-scale operation, placing a listing in the Yellow Pages is an absolute necessity.

This requires installing a business telephone, which is equally important if starting the business from home. Calling for service and having a child, for example, answer the phone will kill any interest a potential client may have.

Check with the Yellow Page Directory Advertising Representative of the telephone company to find out when the directory in your area is published. Since they come out at different times during the year depending on the region, it may be necessary to develop a supplemental newspaper advertising or other promotional campaign.

If, for example, you are planning to open for business in August and the phone book in your area comes out in March, you do not want to lose eight months of valuable exposure to prospective clients by doing nothing during that period of time.

Direct Mail

Another way to target specific markets is through direct mail using brochures, flyers, and other materials outlining your lingerie products and detailing the benefits of using your operation. These days direct mail is a more expensive proposition because of postage, but if you mail only to select groups or zip codes within your city to pull the best response, it can be worthwhile.

Mailing lists, broken down by zip codes, income brackets and other specific factors, can be purchased inexpensively from some printers, even small print shops in your city, advertising agencies, local publications and mailing list brokers, all of which are listed in the Yellow Pages.

If you do institute a direct mail program, be sure to send regular announcements to those who've responded to ads in the past but didn't buy your goods or use your service.

Circumstances frequently change, and sending reminders that you are still in business offering quality service at a fair price is sure to result in response at some point.

Just be aware that the average return for direct mail is between 2% and 5% and don't expect the phone to ring off the hook every time you send a mailing. Consistency is the important factor here.

Specialty Items

Specialty advertising serves as an effective reminder. Specialty advertising refers to the matches, pens, key chains and similar items that have a company's name printed on them . . . every time you use the item, you think about the firm, even if it is subconscious.

Investigate the kind of items you can have printed by visiting a specialty advertising representative (listed in the telephone book under "Advertising"). Notepads, pens, pencils, and desk calendars are among your best forms of specialty advertising.

Classified Ads

Don't underestimate the power of classified ads. Many major corporations utilize the classifieds even though they have sizable budgets available for display advertising. There are several reasons for this:

1) The classifieds are an extremely reliable testing ground for new products, services, and ideas. Although it's true that people who typically "read" the classifieds are a different group from those who scan display ads, they are considered to be responsive and, therefore, can give you a very good idea of whether or not you have placed your ad in the appropriate publication.

2) A short, well-written classified placed in the right publication and under the proper category can be a low-cost method of advertising that guarantees solid returns.

3) If a company is trying to establish a mailing list, a classified ad that features an "Inquiry" statement, such as "Send name and address for free details (or a brochure)," is a good way to build up a file of qualified buyers' names. And they can be considered qualified buyers because it takes time, energy and the cost of a postage stamp for them to get your free information. By writing to you they have stated their interest.

4) Classified ads are inexpensive, ranging from 50 cents to $15 per word, depending on the publication. With careful planning, you should be able to get broad-based coverage without putting a dent in your operating capital.

Sample Classified Advertisement:

> **DESIGNER LINGERIE DIRECT TO YOUR HOME!**
> Get the best selection of low cost, designer lingerie delivered right to your door! Teddies, bras, panties, lotions and much more. Send for your free deluxe catalog to shop from the privacy of your home. Mary Ardmore Lingerie, P.O. Box 123, Dayton, OH 22222, or call (101) 555-1234.

Display Advertising

As with all types of advertising, it is important to define your market when getting ready to place a display ad. Your main goal should be to select a publication that will reach the audience you want and then create a specific ad that appeals to that target group.

To Write or Not to Write?

Writing display ad copy is not for the inexperienced. Although it is possible to learn how to put ideas and words together that will get the results you desire, it is recommended that you hire a copywriter if you have any qualms about producing an ad.

However, if you are confident that you can develop your own ad, remember that it must generate interest through the use of carefully planned words and design.

When planning your ad, keep the following elements in mind:

a) **Visibility.** Your ad may well be surrounded by many others, so make sure it immediately attracts the reader's attention.

b) **Boldness.** Use large art and/or a bold headline as a focal point.

c) **Simplicity.** Don't overwhelm the reader with too many fine details. The ad's main point is lost and so is the reader's attention. This is particularly true in a small ad.

d) **White space.** Just because you have, say, a 4 x 6 inch space to work with, it isn't necessary to fill it up with graphics. White space is a necessary component in assuring your ad will be read.

e) **Use legible typestyles.** The easiest to read are Times Roman and Bookman (the type used in this business guide), which are known as serif typefaces because of the tiny strokes at the tops and bottoms of the letters. San serif (without strokes) type such as Helvetica are okay for ads containing few words, but are difficult for the eye to follow when there is a lot of text. Also, be sure that the type is large enough—generally nothing smaller than 10 point type should be used.

Design and Typesetting

It isn't necessary to be a great artist to create an ad, especially these days with the availability of impressive graphic materials, including cut-out and transfer (press-on) letters in different type faces, symbols, borders and design ideas through graphic art supply companies, such as Formatt and Chartpak. Also, most word processors contain computer graphics that can really dress up your ad at a low cost.

> *Advertising is the greatest art form of the 20th Century.*
>
> *Marshall McLuhan*

If you feel uncomfortable about laying out your ad so it has eye appeal, consider hiring an art student to handle the job for a prearranged fee or as a school assignment (talk with the head of the art department to see if they have a work/study for credit program). Just be sure to review the student's work prior to making a commitment.

Also, check with the advertising department of the newspaper or magazine you are planning to advertise in. There may be graphic artists or designers on staff who will work on the layout for you. In fact, there still are newspapers in the country that offer full services, from ad concept to design work, at minimal charge to clients.

Publications work on tight deadlines so be sure you start the process early enough to get a proof copy of your ad back in time to make any corrections. You can imagine the frustration of seeing your ad appear with the wrong address. Although the publication would probably do a "make-good" for you and run a corrected ad at no charge, the damage has already been done. The final responsibility for the ad rests on you, so plan ahead.

Tracking Ad Response

Some customers will tell you that they saw your ad and might even let you know what they liked or disliked about it. They will probably be in the minority, however, so you must develop methods for determining if your advertising is working for you.

One very simple way is to include a coupon for something in the ad and to count the number of coupons you get within a certain test period after the ad runs. There is one major problem with this, however. Even the most well-intentioned people often cut coupons, file them away in a "safe" place and totally forget about them.

So, although you will be able to gauge response to some degree, be aware that many of the people who come into or call your business have probably seen the coupon, but simply mislaid it or are not the kind of folks who use them.

Predicting Response

There is a standardized formula in advertising that provides a barometer for predicting how much response can be expected from either a display or classified ad. The formula states that you will see 1/2 of the total responses from an ad within a certain period of time after receiving your first inquiry or order. For an ad to run in a daily newspaper, the period of time is 3 days; for a weekly newspaper or magazine, it is 6 days; the period is roughly 15 days for a monthly publication, and within 25 days when running in a bi-monthly. Although there are exceptions, this provides a base from which to track response.

Determining Your Cost per Thousand (CPM)

The CPM equation helps you develop a cost-effective campaign. Basically, it tells you what your ad cost per 1,000 readers will be.

Most publications will provide a CPM comparison upon request (some include it in their media kits), but you can easily figure it out for yourself with just a few facts from publications you are exploring as advertising vehicles.

For convenience sake, CPM equations are typically based on the rate of a full-page black and white ad. You simply divide the full-page rate by the thousands of the overall circulation. It's important that you get the circulation, not the readership, as magazines and newspapers typically claim that their readership is 2 to 50% higher because of "pass-along" of the publication to friends.

For example, if a certain newspaper is charging $2,000 for a full-page ad and they claim their true circulation is 200,000, you will be paying $10 per 1,000 readers for your ad space. Another specialized publication's full-page rate may be $1,000 with a circulation of 50,000. The cost per

1,000 readers will be much higher— $20 per 1,000, but it might be worth it if, for example, you have a unique product or service that is geared to an exclusive market.

Benefits of Paid Circulation

It is also important to know that publications with a paid circulation generally have a readership that is more inclined to respond to advertising. This is because of the simple fact that they are a captive audience who have taken the time to order the publication. This is especially valuable if you ever have a product or service that you're planning to market through mail order.

You can find circulation, readership demographics, advertising rates and other important information about a number of publications (especially those with national distribution) through Standard Rate and Data (SR&D) or the Ayer Directory of Publications (and their monthly updates), available through the research desk at your local library.

Recently, the Advertising Research Foundation and the Association of Business Publishers conducted a study to determine the impact of advertising on the sale of products.

Several different products were used for the study and each was advertised for a 12-month period in an appropriate publication. The results were interesting, but not surprising to anyone who has ever utilized a solid advertising campaign in promoting their business.

- More advertising meant more sales.
- Determining results from an ad campaign generally took 4 to 6 months. (One or two insertions does not indicate viable results.)
- Color in advertisements dramatically increased response and sales.

- A well-developed ad campaign kept on working for a year and sometimes even longer in publications with a high "keep" appeal.

Knowledge and belief in your service, faith in yourself and respect for your customers are the keys to successfully building your future. As you go about starting up and establishing your business, remember the word "profit."

Promotion and Public Relations

Informing the public about your business through the use of business cards, brochures, mailing pieces, and specialty items such as desk calendars, pens, and note pads imprinted with your company name, is a form of advertising that is known as promotion.

The things you can do over and above your paid advertising and promotion that help build your image and keep your business in the public consciousness are referred to as public relations. It is a fine line in terminology, but can make or break your business if not addressed.

There are many clever ways to extend the effectiveness of your advertising and promotional dollars, as illustrated in the following examples.

A Little Creativity Goes a Long Way

The owner of a pet grooming business leaves a business card and a brochure featuring a 20% discount coupon everywhere he goes. When he is running errands, he always takes a handful of brochures with him to hand to store clerks, gas station attendants and waitpersons he runs into along the way.

If he sees a car with a dog in it, or one with a bumper sticker announcing the owners' affection for their pet, he slips a brochure under the windshield wiper. Does it work? Absolutely. He claims that 45% of his new business is from the recipients of his handouts and the majority of them become regular customers.

Another business owner who operates a small walking tour service in her beachside town sends out a one-page quarterly newsletter featuring historical and other facts about the area to everyone who has ever taken the tour. She includes a $10 coupon that can be redeemed by former clients or their guests.

She states that many of her clients are local residents who send their out-of-town visitors on her walking tour, simply because she makes sure they are aware that she is still in business and generates enthusiasm through the newsletter.

Charity Tie-ins

Other ideas you might consider include promoting humanitarian outreach. For example, for every ten referrals to your service, you donate a predetermined amount of money to a local charity. You can easily keep track of their purchases by punching a hole at the edge of a card designed by you or your printer strictly for that purpose.

> *Advertisements contain the only truths to be relied on in a newspaper.*
>
> *Thomas Jefferson*

When you are ready to present the check to the particular charity, make sure the chairperson of the organization is going to be available to accept it and be sure to contact the local press and invite them to the "event." In most cases, they will give you free coverage.

Reminder Cards

Sending regular "thinking-of-you" cards to your past and present clientele is especially effective with service businesses. Again, it assures the customer that you are friendly, reliable and successful—a real plus for your credibility.

Networking

Check out local business-owners groups and the chamber of commerce in your area. Pay your membership dues and join as many as possible. Membership offers you the opportunity to meet people who might use your service, and will, at bare minimum, tell others about you once they know you, feel comfortable and understand what you are offering. You will also be given a listing in the group's directory, generally under your specific category. And, as is so often the case, the members are prone to supporting others involved with their group. It is quite possible that members with compatible businesses will put a stack of your cards or brochures on their counter or in their referral file. In return, you may be able to promote their businesses to your customers. This is the true meaning of "networking."

The directory also gives you bonafide access to an instant mailing list, which you can use to send out promotional flyers or brochures. Participating in their events and the willingness, for example, to speak at functions about your area of specialization will let people know that you are community-minded. This involvement will work to project a positive image for you and your business.

Customer Service

One of the most overlooked areas in promoting business is the impression we create when dealing with customers.

The ageless philosophy that the customer comes first and is always right has, it seems, gotten lost in the shuffle in these days of fast-paced, fast-buck dealings from Main Street to Wall Street.

As a small business owner, it is guaranteed that customers will flock to you if you make them feel important. It is as easy as greeting them warmly (instruct your employees, if you have them, to do the same), maintaining a courteous attitude and inviting them to come back soon—even if they have not purchased anything.

Word travels fast and if you create an atmosphere that makes each and every person you deal with feel like the only person in the world, you can be sure they will tell their friends and neighbors.

> *The advertisement is one of the most interesting and difficult of modern literary forms.*
>
> *Aldous Huxley*

Free Publicity

Free publicity also comes under the category of public relations. This includes articles and interviews in newspapers and magazines or coverage on radio and television, featuring interesting or unusual facts about you and your business.

As any newspaper reporter or talk show host will tell you, everybody has a story to tell. The key is to get the media to zero in on yours and make it available to the public. If you have trouble deciding on a unique angle for your story, invite several friends over for a brainstorming session to create a newsworthy item.

Use your imagination to explore the creative possibilities of your business venture. And then look at your personal story. Perhaps you have completely switched fields with your new business. That represents a story angled toward risk-taking. Maybe you have successfully turned a hobby into a business venture, or created a unique product or developed a new twist on an old theme.

These all qualify as human interest stories. Newspaper and magazine editors love them—almost as much as their readers enjoy them.

Once you have your story angle, call the managing editor or the feature editor of the newspaper. Give him or her a brief description of who you are and what business you are in. Tell them you will be sending out a press release and would be happy to arrange an interview at their convenience.

Invite them to visit your place of business and get a firsthand look at what you are doing and how you're doing it. Do the same with program directors or talk show hosts at regional television and radio stations, offering your availability.

If, on the first attempt, your presentation fails to result in an article, follow up in three to six months, possibly with a new story angle. In the meantime, however, send out regular press releases announcing new developments with your business—the grand opening, special events, details on your business philosophy, extra services and features. Even if they don't run a full story on you alone, there is a good likelihood they will include you in a feature story about local entrepreneurs or people in similar businesses.

An Effective Ad Campaign

All of the methods outlined above, along with others you will develop, keep your name in the consumer's mind. The effectiveness of an advertising/publicity campaign can be measured by conducting a simple marketing survey with new customers. Make it standard practice to ask them where they heard about you and your business.

Keep a tally of the responses in a notebook. A periodic review will give you hints of where to allocate future advertising funds. If, for example, the majority of your customers are being drawn from your direct mailings to potential clients, keep them going on a steady basis. The same principle applies to Yellow Pages display ads, specialty ads or word-of-mouth advertising.

The justification for investing in advertising and promotion is time. If you attempted to contact all of the people who read ads and press release material in newspapers or those who listen to talk shows, you would never have time to conduct your business . . . you would be too busy recruiting.

It can't be stressed enough: Time is money. As a small business owner, you will want to devote as much attention as possible to the production end of your venture and let your advertising and promotion work to bring in the customers.

California Mart - 110 E. 9th Street LA, CA 90079

20

RESOURCES

Wholesalers, Manufacturers & Suppliers

Bali Company Corporate Offices
P.O. Box 5100, Winston-Salem, NC 27113
(910) 519-6053

Sidney Bernstein & Son Lingerie, Inc.
135 Madison Avenue, 11th Floor, New York, NY 10016
(212) 679-4270

213- 680- 2252   A.624

Boutique Industries, Inc.
40 East 34th Street, New York, NY 10016
(212) 679-2270

Chic Lingerie Company
693 High Lane, Redondo Beach, CA 90278
(800) 521-2442

D&D Fashions, Inc./Intimate Fashions
15 East 32nd Street, New York, NY 10016
(212) 686-1530

Fruit of the Loom, Inc.
1101 Greensburg Road, Campbellville, KY 42718
(502) 789-4333

Glencraft Lingerie
38 East 32nd Street, 10th Floor, New York, NY 10016
(212) 689-5990

Goddess Bra
156 Porter Street, Boston, MA 02128
(617) 569-3000
www.goddessbra.com

Intime of California, Inc.
1865 Cordova Street, Los Angeles, CA 90007
(213) 735-1131

Jockey International, Inc.
2300 60th Street, Kenosha, WI 53140
(414) 658-8111

Lady Ester Lingerie Corporation
404 East 10th Street, Berwick, PA 18603
(717) 752-4521

Matis Lingerie, Inc.
River Street, Susquehanna, PA 18847
(717) 853-3140

National Corset Supply House
3240 East 26th Street, Vernon, CA 90023
(800) 421-9359

New Holland Lingerie
Ridge Avenue, Reamstown, PA 17567
(215) 267-5282

Rohr Lingerie, Inc.
209 Dunn Avenue, Old Forge, PA 18518
(717) 562-1902

Tom & Jerry, Inc.
131 West 33rd Street, Suite 1001, New York, NY 10001
(800) 843-6701

Triangle Lingerie Corporation
148 Madison Avenue, Room 401, New York, NY 10016
(212) 725-2585

Val Mode Lingerie, Inc.
P.O. Box 70, Bridgeton, NJ 08302
(609) 451-7800
213-614-0556

Other Catalogs & Brochures

Victoria's Secret
P.O. Box 16589, Columbus, OH 43216
(800) 888-8200

Frederick's of Hollywood, Inc.
6608 Hollywood Blvd., Los Angeles, CA 90028
(213) 466-5151

Fame Time/California Mart
110 East Ninth Street, Suite B-792, Los Angeles, CA 90079
(800) 669-4971

The Xandria Collection
P.O. Box 31039, San Francisco, CA 94131

Catalog Printers & Graphic Designers

Printing Industries of America (PIA) should be able to provide you with a good list of printers in your area well suited to print what you need. You can reach them at:
100 Daingerfield Road, Alexandria, VA 22314
(703) 519-8100

Graphic Arts Technical Foundation (GATF) should be able to provide you with a good list of graphic artists or production designers in your area well suited to produce what you need. You can reach them at:
4615 Forbes Avenue, Pittsburg, PA 15213
(412) 621-6941

Catalog Production References

Production for the Graphic Designer
by James Craig, © 1990 Watson-Guptill Publications, New York, NY
ISBN# 0-8230-4416-5

Printing Technology
by J. Adams, D. Faux, L. Reiber, © 1988 Delmar Publishers, Inc., Albany, NY
ISBN# 0-8273-2775-7

Invoicing, Accounting & Shipping Software

The PC Zone/Mac Zone
15815 SE 37th Street, Bellevue, WA 98006-1800
PC (800) 258-2088
Macintosh (800) 248-0800

PC Connection/Mac Connection
6 Mill Street, Marlow, NH 03456
(800) 800-1111 for both PC & Macintosh software

Commercial Shipping Companies

Airborne Express
(800) 548-6080

Federal Express
(800) 654-0920

United Parcel Service
(800) 742-5877

Associations

Advertising Mail Marketing Association
1333 F St NW, Suite 710, Washington, DC 20004

American Apparel Manufacturing Association
2500 Wilson Blvd, Suite 301, Arlington, VA 22201

American Production & Inventory Control Association
500 W Annandale Road, Fall Church, VA 22046

American Wholesale Marketers Association
1128 16th Street NW, Washington, DC 20036

Apparel Retailers of America
2011 "I" Street NW, Suite 300, Washington, DC 20006

General Reference Books & Periodicals

AT&T 800-number information. Call 1-800-272-0400. *"Financial Studies of the Small Business,"* Financial Research Associates, P.O. Box 7708, Winter Haven, FL 33883

"A Consumer's Guide to Telephone Service," Consumer Information Center, Pueblo, CO 81009

Bacon's Publicity Checker: A comprehensive listing of every major newspaper in the United States and Canada. Available through the Research Desk at your local library.

Encyclopedia of Associations. Published annually by Gale, Detroit. Available through the Research Desk at your local library.

Encyclopedia of Business Information Sources: Published periodically by Gale, Detroit.

National Five-Digit ZIP and Post Office Directory, Address Information Center, 6060 Primacy Parkway, Memphis, TN 38188-9980.

Roget's Thesaurus in Dictionary Form (Synonyms and antonyms)

Superintendent of Documents, Government Printing Office, Washington, DC, 20402 (Request listing of publications)

Tax Guide for Small Businesses. Internal Revenue Service Publication #334. Published annually. Available from local IRS office.

Ulrich's International Periodicals Directory. Comprehensive listing of major magazines and newspapers. Available through the Research Desk at your local library.

Webster's New Collegiate Dictionary, Published by G & C Merriam Company, Springfield, MA.

"*Where to Find Business Information*," by David Brownstone and Gorton Carruth. (Publisher: John Wiley & Sons, New York)

Small Business Associations & Government Agencies

American Marketing Association, 250 South Wacker Drive, Chicago, IL, 60606-5819 (Marketing publications available to non-members.)

Bureau of the Census, Washington, DC, 20233. (Statistical data)

Copyright Office, Library of Congress, 101 Independence Avenue SE, Washington, DC 20559 (Information on copyrighting written and visual materials.)

Council of Better Business Bureaus, 4200 Wilson Blvd.Suite 800, Arlington, VA. 22203 (Ask for a listing of their "Booklets on Wise Buying.")

Dun & Bradstreet, 299 Park Avenue, New York, NY, 10171. (Send for the booklet "This is Dun & Bradstreet," an overview of publications and services.)

International Franchise Association, 1350 New York Avenue NW, Suite 900, Washington, DC, 20005. (Regulation and information on franchises.)

Minority Business Development Agency, Office of Public Affairs, Department of Commerce, Washington, DC 20230.

National Association for the Self-Employed, P.O. Box 612067, DFW Airport, Fort Worth, TX, 75261-2067.

National Association of Women Business Owners, 600 South Federal Street, Chicago, IL, 60605.
National Federation of Independent Business, 150 West 20th Avenue, San Mateo, CA, 94403.

National Insurance Consumers Organization, P.O. Box 3243, Merryfield, VA 22116-3243. (Send self-addressed stamped envelope for free booklet, "Buyer's Guide to Insurance.")

National Minority Business Council, Inc., 235 East 42 St., New York, NY 10017. (Quarterly newsletter for small & minority business.)

National Small Business United, 1155 15th Street NW Suite 910, Washington, DC, 20005. (Send for info on federal legislation for small businesses.)

National Trade and Professional Associations of the United States. Available through the Research Desk at your local library.

Occupational Safety & Health Administration (OSHA), Department of Labor, Washington, DC 20210. (Employment regulations.)

Office of Information and Public Affairs, U.S. Department of Labor, 200 Constitution Ave NW, Washington, DC, 20210 (Request publications list regarding employment.)

Small Business Administration, 1441 L Street NW, Washington, DC, 20416. (For booklets and information on the Service Corps of Retired Executives — SCORE.)

INDEX